MOTHER AND ME
A Cold War Boyhood

ROY KERSHAW

*To the memory
of my mother Martha
who always stuck to her principles*

Thanks to author Deb Tyler-Bennett for advice on structure of the book and extensive editing. Also to Deb's Workers' Educational Association writing class who provided useful observations and constructive criticism.

To my son Paul Kershaw who helped design the front cover and formatted the book.

To brother Len Kershaw who helped find photographs, bmd certificates, newspaper articles and other family records.

CONTENTS

Preface		*1*
Foreword - Martha and Harry		*4*
1	*A Political Primer*	*13*
2	*Travels with My Mother*	*30*
3	*Dedicated Follower of Fashion*	*49*
4	*Music, Music, Music*	*57*
5	*All You Need is Love*	*70*
6	*Don't Drink and Drive!*	*97*
7	*Education, Education, Education*	*116*
8	*Politics, Politics, Politics*	*133*
9	*Transition*	*148*
10	*Reconciliation*	*160*

Preface

The 1950s and 60s witnessed the heights of the Cold War between Eastern Communist and Western Capitalist Nations. International crises brought many confrontations between the USSR and the USA, as well as Britain. The Korean War, Suez Crisis and Hungarian Revolution in the 50s. Fall of the Berlin Wall, Cuban Missile Face-off and Prague Spring in the 60s. Straddling both decades were the Vietnam War and the Nuclear Arms Race.

In Britain, communists and the *Daily Worker* usually took the USSR's side in these conflicts, precipitating direct hostility with government, media and most of the public. Added to these were many industrial disputes between unions and employers, both public and private, as well as fear that the Communist Party, with support from Russia, was trying to ferment revolution in the UK. 'Reds under the Bed' was the cry.

For the son of a communist trade union leader father and radical mother (most of whose family were members of the Party), it was a difficult period. The media, in all its forms – newspapers, television and radio – constantly attacked communism. Whether it be accusations of inciting and prolonging strikes, supporting revolutionary movements in the Colonies, or perpetuating the nuclear arms race, communists were continually vilified. Being first in my family to go to grammar school, I also faced animosity from pupils and teachers alike, though usually managing to counter intermittent taunting.

In the 1950s, communism seemed to be advancing around the globe. As well as communist regimes in the USSR, China and Eastern Europe, insurgencies in Malaya, Korea, French Indochina, South America and Cuba were bringing communism ever closer. The World Map was turning Red. Launch of Sputnik in 1957, followed by Yuri Gagarin as the first cosmonaut in 1961, put the USSR ahead in the Space Race. Success at the Olympics, with communist countries winning most of the medals, apparently showed the superiority of socialist ideology. But it was all illusory. Communism was, in fact, crumbling from the inside. The Sino-Soviet split in the 1960s was followed by successful anti-Soviet uprisings in several eastern European countries in the 1980s. Fall of the Berlin Wall in 1989 heralded the collapse of communism, finalised by dissolution of the Soviet Union in 1991. In Britain, the Communist Party underwent numerous splits, finally being disbanded in 1991.

The atrocities of the Soviet Regime began to be exposed following Khrushchev's 'Secret Speech' in 1956 when the then President denounced Stalin Purges. Brutal collectivization of peasant farms; mass deportation of ethnic minorities; religious persecution; show trials; massacres of opponents to the Regime were all well documented. Solzhenitsyn's *The Gulag Archipelago* removed any doubts as to the authenticity of the reports. Many British communists left the Party as a result of these exposures, but many didn't, the latter often closing their eyes to the abominations, believing it to be exaggerated capitalist propaganda. Some even followed the doctrine of 'the end justifies the means'. Cynically 'You can't make an omelet without breaking eggs.'

Despite the communist system and ideology being totally discredited, especially in the Soviet Union, this didn't mean that individual communists could be written off as 'evil'. Many had joined the Party dedicated to building a better society worldwide. They worked unselfishly to promote the interests of the working class and to bring an end to war, injustice, hunger and human suffering. The American author, Howard Fast, even after he had broken with communism, wrote of the tiny Communist Party of the USA: 'that never in so small a group have I seen so many pure souls, so many gentle and good people, so many men and women of utter integrity.' My own experience echoes these sentiments. Mother and Father clung to communist ideology longer than most. To them, communism was as much a religion as a political system. Despite increasing evidence of its failure, they still retained 'faith' in socialist ideals. My Father died in 1985, avoiding much of the calamitous end of communism. Mother passed away in 1991, cutting herself off from the real world, unable to face almost total disintegration of her 'Utopian Vision'.

The 1950s and 60s also witnessed huge social and cultural changes, particularly for the working class. Increased prosperity and spending power, and advances in technology and science, led to teenagers

Preface

breaking free from previous generations in fashion, leisure pursuits, music and sexual mores. Mother resisted most of these changes, clinging to impossibly high social and cultural norms. This inevitably led to clashes between a highly principled mother and a son eager to taste the fruits of a more permissive society. Educational opportunity was another big change in the 1950s. Secondary education had been made available and compulsory at the end of the previous decade, split largely into secondary modern and selective grammar schools. Though the vast majority of working-class children went to the former, there were still opportunities to enter the grammar school system via 11-plus examinations. Mother grabbed the opportunity for her son with both hands, relentlessly pushing and encouraging me to good 'O-level' and 'A-level' results and a place at university. Since many of my friends had gone to secondary modern school, leaving at 15, there were constant skirmishes as Mother tried to break these links, despite her own working-class credentials.

A 'relationship cold war' was added to the 'political cold war'.

FOREWORD

Martha and Harry

'Your Dad carried the tiny white coffin on his shoulder, slowly trudging from the front door of the family home. They lived in Barnoldswick at the time. It was a mournful scene; tears and pained faces. Everyone was there, all the sisters, brothers, grandparents and close friends. Your Mum was unable to speak, eyes cast down to the rain spattered pavement. Stoic, as always.'

Uncle Hubert reminisces with great sadness in his voice, remembering the funeral of my long lost brother, Robert Allan who was born on 13th of September 1933, passing away on 6th March 1934 at just 5 months old. I remember these dates well because Mother would say every year: 'Bobby would have been 22 today' or whatever the relevant age.

Mother was second eldest of six sisters and a brother whilst Father had two sisters and two brothers. Robert was first born of any Smith or Kershaw sibling, so the bereavement was particularly difficult to contemplate. Mother always said he died of 'an in-running ear' though the death certificate records 'Osteomyelitis of Femur'. Being well before the NHS, health services were rudimentary; few maternity hospitals, with babies usually being born at home. Probably nothing could have been done to save Robert, but no doubt both parents felt some responsibility; gnawing, though mistaken, feelings of guilt.

The result was almost obsessive care of her other two sons; Len, born in 1936 and Roy, born in 1944. A dose of Coxes Extra Strong Bronchial Emulsion at the first sign of a cold or cough. Only the best foods; butter, not margarine; Chanel Island full cream milk; eggs every morning; brown farmhouse loaves; fruit always available. When leaving the house: 'Put a coat on, Roy. It's cold outside.' An irritating nightly reminder: 'Remember to clean your teeth' (Mother had fallen and broken two front teeth at an early age). There were many visits to the doctor whenever a health problem arose, however small;

Martha and Harry

usually involving long, long waits at the surgery: 'We'll wait for Doctor Edie, Doctor Spears doesn't give enough time, you're in and out in a flash', Mother would say. I was encouraged to take part in sports for physical wellbeing, music for mental wellbeing. I didn't miss a single day of school throughout my infant, junior, and most of my secondary school career.

* * *

Martha Smith was born in Barnoldswick (Barlick), a small North West cotton town on the border of Yorkshire and Lancashire; on the Tyke side. The year, 1905. Parents, Ellen and Jud Smith, were both weavers living in a two up, two down, back-to-back terraced house, built for textile workers at the height of the industrial revolution. First born was also a girl, Bessie. Four other sisters followed; Annie, Ida, Mary and Clarice. An only son, Frank, was the youngest. All of them were to become textile workers, mainly weavers.

The rented family home, reached from a narrow cobbled street, is built of solid Yorkshire stone, blackened by smoke belched out from a myriad of mill chimneys. A flagged, gated yard leads to the front door, in fact the only door. In the yard is an outside 'tippler privy' with two 'guzundas' (chamber pots) on guard for use inside the house. The house has small, multi-paned windows with flimsy curtains, too thin to keep out sunlight during the day. Not that much light penetrates the closely built properties. A wooden 'front' door, painted dull brown, leads straight into the kitchen where patches of oilcloth partially cover a stone-slabbed floor. Shallow slop-stone sink, with single cold water tap, is used for washing pots; and people. A tin bath hangs on the wall, available for laundering both clothes and children. Iron pans and copper kettle dangle from whitewashed walls on hooks inexpertly hammered in by father Jud. Long-handled wooden brooms lie in the corner, along with well-worn scrubbing brushes and 'donkey stones'.

The living room's dark and dismal. Worn, faded damask covers a horse-hair filled couch and two armchairs, taking up much of the space. A dresser along one wall, with glass display cabinets, exhibits a seldom used china tea set and flowered vases. The room's dominated by an open range; a great big exhibition of polished iron with hob grate in the middle, oven on one side, iron tank for hot water on the other.

The room's dimly lit by gas mantles, two in wall mountings and another two in an elaborate glass 'gasolier' in the middle of the room, but only when pennies are available to feed the meter. Often they're not, candlelight then having to suffice. Sticky brown strips of fly paper, dangling from the gasolier, trap only some of the houseflies and bluebottles on hot summer days. Two spartan bedrooms are small; adequate when only parents and two children are to be accommodated, but entirely inadequate for a family of eight. Martha and Bessie often have to sleep downstairs with as many as four in a bed upstairs, sleeping 'tops and tails'. There's no heating in the house, except for a fire in the open range, which can only be lit when money's available to buy coal slack or coke. Upstairs is particularly cold, winter causing ice not only on the outside of windows, but also inside the bedrooms. 'Pegged rugs', made from strips of old clothes, bring a little comfort and warmth. Finances don't stretch to gaslights upstairs, only candles.

On the day after 'pay-day' bread and marg are on the kitchen table instead of the usual dripping, with a tin of beans for supper. Sometimes, on Saturday night, there's cod from the fish shop. 'Any fish you like for a tanner' shouts the fishmonger as he tries to clear his stock. Nestles milk is often substituted for cow's milk. Unpopular with the Smith sisters are black pudding, tripe and pigs trotters. 'They're good for you' Ellen says, unconvincingly. Special treats at the weekend include small white basins of cooked peas from a cauldron, bought from a 'pay 'oil' in town.

Martha, like many other children in working-class households, begins working at twelve years old in the 'Half-Time System'. This means going to school mornings (though little is taught - or learnt), and to the weaving shed afternoons. Wearing shawl and straw hat, Martha joins the many other young workers as they hurry to the mill. Jet black hair, severely pinned back, is largely hidden by the wide brimmed straw boater. The sound of clog irons echo on paving stones. Children have to contribute to family finances as soon as possible, working as many as 30 hours per week on low pay. Whilst Ellen and Jud operate four looms each the wolf's kept from the door, but if either is sick, or trade reduces the number of working looms, items have to be pawned, or money sought from door to door loan sharks.

Jud's involved in opening a co-operative store in the town; principles of democratic member control, sale of unadulterated foods and concern for the community appealing to his socialist convictions. The store's non-profit making, returning any surplus as a dividend. The 'Divi' makes a significant contribution to family income at the end of the year.

'We're goin' te ger everythin' from t'co-op store now' declares Jud to a receptive family audience. 'No goin' te that capitalist corner shop. They're cheats. Put chalk int' flour and tamper wit' scales.'

Jud and Ellen also join the newly formed Weavers Union. Weavers work 55½ hours per week in appalling factory conditions. Air in the weaving shed's hot and humid, thick with cotton dust. There are frequent accidents from flying shuttles, and thunderous noise from hundreds of looms makes it impossible to hear each other's voices. Wages are low, often reduced further by a system of fines if faults in the cloth are found. Deductions also for lateness, even a few minutes. Work starts as early as six in the morning with a half hour for breakfast at half-past seven and a one hour lunch break at one o'clock. The mill closes down at half-past five whilst Saturday work is from seven in the morning to half-past twelve.

Bessie speaks out at a Union meeting.

'It's *more* than 55½ hours a week working. It takes 15 minutes to walk t't mill, so no time te go 'ome. We've only a bit a' bread fer breakfast; eaten at work, sittin' on a damp floor. Not even 'ot water te mek a cup'a te'. Sometime looms a' stopped 'cos a' problems wit' yarn. When't looms 'er stopped we don't get paid' she protests. 'And what abaht all't deafening noise?'

Martha joins in.

'Ye', on our feet all day. Sweat dripping off, covered in cotton. We only get paid fer t' length a' cloth weaved. It's not fair. When mothers ger 'ome they've te start work agin, making meals fer t'family, doin't washin' and cleanin'. Don't finish 'til ten at night. Up again at five int' mornin'. We've got te do summat abaht it'. A murmur of agreement ripples round the meeting. 'Ere, Ere'.

Bessie, and husband Harold, are particularly active. They think nothing of cycling 30 miles to the Socialist Hall in Openshaw, near Manchester. Pedalling through the Rossendale Valley, with its textile mills and gritstone terraced houses, they skirt the cotton towns of

Rawtenstall, Oldham and Rochdale. Taking part in demonstrations, and distributing leaflets at weaver's strikes, eventually leads to arrest and imprisonment in Preston Gaol for Bessie. 'Agitation and circulating pamphlets calculated to cause mutiny' are the charges. Martha, Bessie and other Party members also collect and deliver the *Daily Worker* door-to-door, to factories and union members when the Newspaper Wholesalers Federation refuses to distribute the Paper.

Bessie and Martha also join the Labour Party, but soon become disillusioned. In 1933 there's a by-election in Skipton constituency, which includes Barlick. A local weaver, Jim Rushton, is candidate for the Communist Party. His charismatic personality and radical speeches even include quotes from Shelley's *'The Masque of Anarchy'*:

'Rise, like lions after slumber
in unvanquishable number.
Shake your chains to earth like dew
which in sleep had fallen on you:
Ye are many – they are few!'

The Smith Clan are enormously attracted by this working-class hero, actively supporting his campaign, leafleting outside factory gates, marching in support of weaver's strikes, heckling at Conservative hustings. 'Tha' knows nowt' shouts Jud from the back of the hall. Labour and Communist supporters cheer.

But despite enthusiastic campaigning by six well-known, exceptionally good looking Smith siblings Jim gets only 704 votes, compared with over 18 thousand for the successful Tory candidate, and 14 thousand for Labour. 'At least we've made an impact, Comrades' says Jim defiantly. The Communist Party Cabal continues to meet, always finishing with The Rebel Song.

'Come workmen sing a rebel song,
a song of love and hate.
Of love unto the lowly,
and of hatred to the great.
The great who trod our fathers down,
who steal our children's bread.
Whose hands of greed are stretched to rob,

Martha and Harry

the living and the dead

Then sing a rebel song
as we proudly march along.
To end the age long tyranny
that makes for human tears.
Our march is nearer done
with each setting of the sun.
And the tyrants might is passing
with the passing of the years.'

It's at a Union meeting that Martha first encounters Harry who's making an impassioned speech.

'Comrades, we must resist the constant efforts of this Tory Government and Employers to cut wages. Most families are already on the breadline and any further cuts will bring abject poverty to our mothers and children. We must come together to fight the profiteers. Solidarity's what we need!'

Martha's impressed. Harry's wavy, auburn hair and ruddy face are also an attraction. Quite tall, wearing a smart though inexpensive stone-coloured suit, Harry's black rimmed spectacles give him the air of a working-class intellectual. After the meeting, Harry comes over to the Smith sisters. He's attracted by Martha's slim figure outlined by a toned down, below the knee, flapper-style dress. Incongruously the dress is dark blue, not red. 'No doubt made at home' Harry surmises. Her jet black, bobbed hair unusually has curls caressing soft cheeks. He sees dark, flashing eyes and deeply challenging sensuality.

'Haven't I seen you before?' he asks Martha, ignoring the other sisters. 'Aren't you in the Clarion?'

Barlick Clarion's a cycling club, one of the few pastimes available to working-class boys and girls. Clarion members think nothing of cycling miles on a Sunday into the Yorkshire countryside, taking a picnic with them and meeting up with other young people.

'Yes I am. Think I've seen you there' Martha replies encouragingly.
'We're going to Pendle Hill next Sunday. Will you be there?' Harry asks optimistically.

'Yes, I'll be there, but with my sisters Bessie and Ida.'

Harry thanks his lucky stars he almost has a date with such a beautiful girl, even if it is to be chaperoned. His heart sings.

* * *

Harry was born 1907 in Whitewell Bottom, a hamlet nestling in the Rossendale Valley. The small village is near Rochdale, birthplace of the co-operative movement, where most of the Kershaw family live. Mother, Florence, is a weaver, but father, Hubert, has a slightly better job as twister and drawer. Harry's eldest of five children; brothers Hubert and Allan, sisters Pauline and Lona.

Similarly to Martha, Harry's incorporated into the 'Half Time System' at 12 years old. Although meant to contribute to family income, in practice little is earned. Nine months of training, without any pay, then just one loom under the piece work system, yielding little income. Several years to move to four looms with pay in line with industry norms. All earnings are 'tipped up' into family coffers, especially when father and mother are laid off and claiming 'Lloyd George'. To earn spending money, Harry takes on part-time work, the first job being as 'sweeper up', which involves collecting cotton sweepings from around looms and depositing in the waste dump. This is done Friday lunchtimes and after the mills close on Saturday. Next, Harry becomes a 'lather boy'. The many barbers in town not only cut hair, but also shave their clients. Boys are employed to 'lather up' customers before a cut throat razor finishes the shave, hopefully without bloodshed. Working hours are half-past six to eight on two evenings a week and a long shift on Saturday afternoon, finishing at eight in the evening. The job also involves sweeping the shop, making it hard work and long hours after weaving all day, though at two shillings and sixpence a week, it's quite lucrative.

Weavers are paid under what's known as the 'Uniform List', a complicated piece-work system which takes into account not only the length woven, but also the type and quality of the cloth. Just two of ten provisions in the 'Oldham List' give an idea of the complexity of the system:

'For the Reed, give and take for every four Ends in the inch, One Farthing per piece of 25 yards. Three or more Ends in one dent to be

Martha and Harry

paid according to the number of Ends per inch.'
'Fancies, Seven to Twelve Shafts, inclusive, to be paid One Half-penny more than Plain Cloth for 25 yards. Thirteen Shafts One penny more than Plain Cloth for 25 yards.'

Though education's rudimentary, Harry's exceptionally good at arithmetic, making him one of the few weavers (or even employers) who can calculate earnings. He's soon approached by other weavers, mainly women, to help check if their wages are correct; help that's gladly given. They're also encouraged to join the Union. Harry's activities soon come to the attention of the mill boss and he's sacked for 'political agitation'. Being sacked, Harry cannot draw the 'Dole' and he's now on a blacklist, unable to find work. In 1932 Harry goes on a one year working and education visit to the Soviet Union, sponsored by the International Labour Office of the United Nations. He works three days a week in a factory making railway breaking systems (ironically from an American patent and produced under licence), and three days at Moscow University studying politics and economics. In an interview later in life on Radio Blackburn, Harry relates an experience that had greatly strengthened his faith in the communist system.

'One evening, whilst gazing out of my second-storey apartment, I witnessed an amazing scene. Outside was a cobbled road, about half a mile long. Maybe a hundred workers arrived carrying spades, pick axes and other equipment – and singing Russian patriotic and Socialist songs. When I looked out the following morning, the whole road had been asphalted, with concrete pavements down the edge.'

In 1935, Harry's awarded the Tolpuddle Medal for his Union work.

* * *

Now living in Colne, Harry and Martha are married in 1930. Parents had been shocked when Harry announces he's leaving home to get married and, almost in the same breath, that he's been sacked! Martha's still working though, with four looms, now the sole breadwinner. It's uncertain who's to pay 7s 6d for the marriage licence.

At the start of the war Harry trains as a setter-operator on automatic machines at the Royal Ordnance Factory in Alsager where he joins the AEU, becoming a shop steward. After the war, experience gained at ROF enables him to get a skilled job at Rolls Royce Aero Engine Factory in Barlick on a weekly wage of £11.50, far higher than in weaving. Nevertheless, when approached by Colne weavers to become secretary of the union branch, Harry happily agrees, even though his wage will now be only £4.50.

The marriage is as much political as romantic. Both have strongly held socialist convictions; both are members of the Weavers Union; both are committed to the co-operative movement. On other aspects of life there are significant differences though. Harry smokes quite heavily: 'Paying all that money to ruin your health' Martha says with disdain. Harry drinks, though moderately: 'Only pigs drink when they're not thirsty' comments Martha. Harry bets regularly on the horses, his brother Allan being a 'bookie's runner'. Gambling's to be the cause of several family arguments. Martha's a 'militant idealist'; fully subscribed warrior in the Class War. Undeviating hard line views turn some people off: 'Made more Conservatives than Winston Churchill' comments cousin Harvey. Harry's much more of a 'liberal', willing to listen to other points of view and to compromise. He even reads the *Daily Mail* as well as the *Daily Worker*, though the former on the train, not at home. As a union leader, negotiations with the bosses are tough, but he remains on friendly first name terms.

But in the basics, they are as one. Committed to helping others, even when not in their own interests; true to their political ideals; compassionate and caring; and family oriented. A shared vision of a Working-Class Utopia.

CHAPTER 1

A Political Primer

'If you tread on a nick, you'll marry a brick' I whisper to myself whilst hopping and skipping behind Mother, though still managing to keep hold of her hand. There seems no basis or logic for this idiosyncratic saying, except that it rhymes. But dodging the nicks adds challenge to walking or running along the pavement. 'Nicks' are small gaps between the solid, dull bronze-coloured Victorian paving slabs, the aim being to avoid touching them. To my knowledge there's no record of anyone actually marrying a brick!

It's Saturday morning and we hurry towards Skipton Road and the bus stop at the brow of the hill. Unusually for Colne, a typical North West Lancashire cotton town, the weather's dry and hot with waves of heat shimmering from flagstones and cobbles on the streets we cross along the way. Bubbles of tar multiply on newly asphalted main roads which I try to burst; until Mother drags me away. I try spinning round the ornately decorated gas lamp outside the Mayor's house, but again Mother drags me back. Grass verges at the edge of the pavement are overgrown, as are some of the privet hedges fronting generally well kept gardens. Rows of pebble-dashed terraced council houses with identical front doors and windows, painted an identical shade of muddy brown, line the street. Pig bins at the side of the road are beginning to pong in the intense heat.

We pass textile mills, in one of which Mother toils during the week as a weaver. The high, domineering buildings, some of them dating from the industrial revolution, are built of local grey stone. Tall chimneys punctuate the skyline, smoke plumes rising, adding to the dirt and grime blackening factory walls. In his poem *'Jerusalem'* William Blake perhaps has in mind such edifices when he writes of 'dark satanic mills' though on this bright sunny morning they look anything but dark, and certainly not satanic. We hurry past another prominent building, the Co-op grocery store and butchers.

Co-operative stores are omnipresent in the town, as they are in much of Lancashire, the Co-operative Movement having originated in nearby Rochdale, my Father's home town. The store is familiar since I'm sent there to do the weekly family shop, struggling to carry groceries back to our council house at the top of the hill. But, as with everything else, I don't complain – just get on with it.

The weekly shop takes ages. Counter service means the assistant has to fetch every item on the shopping list. A farmhouse loaf, two vanilla slices and two Eccles cakes from the bakery section; potatoes and carrots have to be weighed and bagged in the vegetable section; bacon and cooked meats sliced and wrapped in grease proof paper. Increasing frustration as the full order's slowly completed. 'What's your Co-op number?' asks the assistant as she fills in the 'divi slip'. Mother's number is 4221, but brother Len has just joined the Co-op and has his own number. I'm under pressure to use his. '8609' I reply to the assistant.

As usual, we're in a hurry, though not through any dilatoriness or affectation on Mother's part. Having worked hard all week - forty five hours minimum – in the noisy, unhealthy environment of a weaving shed, Mother has risen early to struggle with the weekly wash, using washtub and mangle; all by hand. She's tired. The relentless drudgery of the cotton mill and never ending housework is taking its toll, though Mother doesn't slow down. Perhaps discontent with this situation was the real catalyst of the women's liberation movement, not concerns about social and sexual freedoms.

We reach the bus stop just as a double-decker omnibus arrives, gaudily painted in primrose and crimson lake. The bus is emblazoned with the grand logo of the newly formed Burnley, Nelson and Colne Joint Transport Committee, reflecting immense civic pride. Climbing on board, I make a move towards stairs leading to the upper deck, though quickly pulled back by Mother. What lies at the top of the stairs is a mystery so I imagine it a den of iniquity where dastardly deeds are done; part of the attraction of ascending the steps. The down to earth reason? Mother doesn't venture to the top deck because smoking's allowed there, so we always go downstairs, even when there are no seats. It's also difficult to see out of the bus windows, adding to the tediousness of a slow, multi-stop journey.

Arriving in Nelson, our neighbouring town, we alight into a crowded,

A Political Primer

bustling street, noisy with the jolly sound of a brass band, and eager gossip of young girls and rowdy youths. It's Gala Day. Most Lancashire mill towns hold these annual events involving parades of church groups, scouts and guides, trade unions, drum bands and Morris Dancers, as well as local dignitaries. A gaudily decorated float carries the town's 'Cotton Queen'. These pretty girls are chosen by the local gala committee to represent the town at various civic functions. Often they aren't the most attractive girls in town, having been chosen by a group of older, staid councillors and local worthies. A main selection criterion insists the girl be seen as wholesome, with a nice smile; and no 'reputation'. The best looking girls in town often don't match up to these prerequisites.

The gala parade hasn't yet started, with various groups assembling in line awaiting the big send-off. A Weavers Union banner is prominent near the front of the Parade. Air Cadets are led by a smart, proud Mace Thrower, launching the mace to incredible heights, though still managing to catch it on its way down; usually. Marching Bands strut along the street; purple uniforms, neatly pleated short skirts, instruments played in strict time, but without melody. Mayors from both Nelson and Colne ride in the official black open-topped limousine, gold mayoral chains glistening in the bright sun. We continue down side streets before stopping outside Silverman Hall, named after the local Labour MP. Mother's wearing a new flowery summer dress, expertly sewn by herself. I'm smart in short grey trousers, a starched short-sleeved white shirt and long grey socks. Good quality, sturdy shoes are well polished. The weather's becoming warmer and warmer with no breeze or shade as my face grows pinker, blond curls beginning to stick to my forehead as sweat trickles down. My fair complexion's a problem in the relentless glare but, without sun cream, I suffer in silence.

It isn't long before a resplendent vehicle comes to a stop at the kerbside. A highly polished, shiny wagon stands there shimmering in the sun, newly painted in a royal shade of maroon. On the back of the wagon sit a dozen boys and girls, about my own age, each waving differently coloured pennants. Stretched across the top of the wagon is a beautifully adorned banner bearing the maxim 'Peace Throughout the World'. The word Peace is repeated on posters fastened to the sides of the vehicle. As a precociously early reader, I'm able to understand the words and phrases, particularly as they're often used at home by my Parents. I can also read the embossed black writing on the cab door of the wagon: **'Colne Co-operative Society, Coal Department'**.

My illusion of a magical chariot vanishes as I realise this is the vehicle that regularly visits our house to deliver coal for our open hearth fire. This is not to disparage the committed enthusiasts who have lovingly cleaned, painted and polished the wagon, making it fit to join the gala procession, so it's still with some pride I'm lifted onto the back of the wagon to join the other children. Each boy and girl has the name of a nation on their pennant, including a preponderance of Eastern European countries. My own pennant's bright red, clearly and artistically printed '**SPAIN**'.

This scene provides a useful visual representation of my family. Father, Harry, is President of Colne and District Co-operative Society. The gala float's sponsored and decorated by the local Communist Party, of which both parents, as well as my wider family, are active and leading members. Harry's also a trade union official, eventually to become General Secretary of the Weavers Amalgamation in Manchester. My family are totally bound up with the socialist left in Britain. In my parent's and many peoples' eyes, the Communist and Labour Parties, Trade Unions, as well as Co-operative Societies, are to be the building blocks of a truly socialist future.

It's not by chance my pennant's coloured 'socialist' red and represents Spain. Only a little more than a decade has passed since the Spanish Civil War. A close friend of my Father, a fellow communist, fought with the International Brigades against the fascist dictator Franco. A military coup against the elected Republican Government in Spain had been supported by Hitler and Mussolini as well as the Catholic Church. Many people, not only on the left, saw the Spanish Civil War as a fight against Fascism, which it undoubtedly was. It was also a fight they hoped would be won, so averting a Second World War. But in 1939 the Franco regime was recognized by France and the UK, so war was inevitable. Later in life I'm jolted into reading more about the Spanish Civil War after seeing the painting *'Guernica'* by Pablo Picasso. This graphic and moving image of death and destruction, caused by German bombing of a defenceless town in Northern Spain, had a major impact on developing pacifist views.

A Political Primer

* * *

I accompany Mother on another campaign; handing out leaflets calling for an end to conscription to the armed forces. We again go by bus, this time to Burnley, there joining other campaigners in the open market on a very busy Saturday. Not being asked or expected to hand out leaflets myself, I try to be as inconspicuous as possible to save myself from acute embarrassment. Motivation for this campaign is anti-militarism, though this is reinforced by knowledge that my older brother, Len, faces National Service in two years time. In the event, conscription didn't end until 1960 so Len, who reached 18 in 1954, was to join the army. Even then, our parent's anti-militarism persisted with Len encouraged to join the Royal Army Medical Core (RAMC) and thus train to save lives rather than take them.

There aren't many takers for the leaflets. 'We wouldn't have won the war with you lot in charge' shouts one angry passer-by. 'Communist scum' shouts another, but Mother doesn't flinch. A woman, still wearing her weaver's apron, comes up and shakes Mother's hand. 'Keep up the good work' she says, encouragingly. Mother is arguing with a military looking man, no doubt an old soldier, as I wander away into the busy open market. Never-ending stalls sell everything under the sun. An Asian trader shouts his wares: 'Chinese towels. Only a quid for a set of five.' Another stall holder's selling tripe, pig's trotters, cow heels, black puddings, elder and sheep's heads. I move along quickly. A toy stall displays Dinky toys but I'm more interested in the small model railway with wind up engine, chugging around a circular track. The next stall sells sweets: pontefract cakes; coconut mushrooms; gobstoppers; sherbet dips; and my own favourite, bull's-eyes. I buy a packet with my last penny.

Mother shouts 'It's time to go. Hurry up or we'll miss the bus. Burnley are playing at home today so we'd better get a move on before the crowds.' There seem to be a lot of leaflets left over; it can't have been a good day, but Mother remains determined.

* * *

The Lancashire and Cheshire District Communist Party Congress is to be held at the Belle Vue Conference Centre in Manchester.

Described as the *'Showground of the World'*, Belle Vue's a vast area including a zoo, amusement park, sports stadium and many other attractions, as well as the conference centre. We arrive on a charabanc hired by Nelson and Colne Communist Party accommodating thirty passengers with me the only child. I follow Mother and Father into the hall where we sit in front seats on the balcony. The hall's full and noisy with excited chatter of enthusiastic and committed delegates. Then there's a hush as the Chairman and District Committee Members come onto the platform. They're mainly white, middle-aged men dressed in slightly dishevelled suits and ties; certainly not the wild-eyed revolutionaries often portrayed in the press. The General Secretary of CPGB, Harry Pollitt, stands up to speak. He's articulate and without the strong Lancashire accent I'm used to. No 'the's trouble at' mill' or 'am gerrin' on't buzz' intonation. The audience is attentive and, at first, quiet, but soon the silence is broken by isolated shouts of 'Ere, Ere' like irregular reports of a farmer's bird scarer. Feeling this to be quite rude, I frown in distaste. Of course this isn't how the speakers understand it as the shouts are expressions of support and agreement by delegates; less intrusive than repeated interruptions by bursts of applause.

Although initially entertained by this new experience, I'm soon bored and restless. Mother senses this, noticing my continual fidgeting and frequent yawns.

'Roy, you can go outside, but don't go far away.'

I make my way out, excitedly looking forward to sampling the pleasures of the *'Showground of the World'*, but after walking round for a while, I'm disillusioned. Most of these pleasures are behind walls and fences, requiring payment to enter and since I haven't any money, I'm deeply disappointed. Continuing to wander in the hope that free entertainment might miraculously appear, suddenly I spot a queue of people at a turnstile where, apparently, entrance is free. Could this be the answer to my dreams? Standing and watching for several minutes, but too shy to ask, I conclude that, indeed, no payment's necessary so, joining the queue, I go through the turnstile. Too late! I'm now outside Belle Vue showground, stranded on the wide pavement. The entrance to free entertainment is in fact the Exit.

What to do? The turnstile's only one way - Out. There's a wide double iron gate further along, but it's heavily locked and too high to

A Political Primer

climb over even if I dare; which I don't. I'm stranded, standing forlorn as an official looking man in an equally official looking uniform comes to the gate and opens it using a bunch of official looking keys. A lorry trundles out, loaded with brightly painted fairground equipment, and turns into the road. Now's my chance to dash back into the showground through the still open gate; but my courage fails. I look pleadingly at the gateman but either he doesn't notice or regards me as just another kid trying to get in for free. Other opportunities arise when gates open again, but innate shyness prevents me asking the gatekeeper to let me in.

It's over an hour later when I spot Mother hurrying towards the gate in panic. Am I in big trouble? I show no emotion as the gates are opened and my hand's firmly gripped, though once through the gate, burst into tears. Mother doesn't admonish me, however, partly through relief that I've been found, and partly through a measure of guilt, having allowed me to leave the conference hall on my own. We arrive back at the charabanc to be met with a warm welcome; no recriminations.

* * *

Another major event during the year, a few weeks before Christmas, is the Daily Worker Bazaar. Silverman Hall's the venue and we arrive early, this time with both Mother and Father. We've bags full of children's clothes, knitwear and soft furnishings that Mother's spent several months making by hand, using her precious Singer sewing machine. The items are added to a vast array of goods for sale, neatly and attractively spread out on trestle tables round the room as well as a square in the middle. Home-made cakes and pies; knitwear; second-hand toys; books; housewares; textiles; gifts; and a huge assortment of bric-a-brac on the white elephant stalls. They make for a dazzling display of merchandise, all donated free by Communist Party members and sympathisers; often made with their own hands. This is dedication to creating, as they see it, a just and equal society. The hall's infused with a welcoming aroma of tea, coffee and pastries, as well as Lancashire hotpot and mushy peas, available during the hectic rush of the forthcoming sale to resuscitate stall holders and customers alike. I look forward to these culinary delights.

The whole room's seasonally decorated with Xmas trimmings and red, blue and yellow fairy lights, plus the essential Christmas tree. A bearded Santa Claus sits in a hastily constructed Grotto in the corner. I look closer; it's Uncle Harold! Someone puts a record on the old, dilapidated gramophone. Through the crackling and popping, words can still be heard:

'Then raise the scarlet standard high,
within its shade we'll live and die.
Though cowards flinch and traitors sneer,
we'll keep the red flag flying here'

Outside, the weather's dismal with angry clouds precipitating an interminable drizzle, though that doesn't dampen the anticipation and excitement of the queue of warmly clad customers awaiting the opening. Although some of the crowd are dedicated socialists coming to support a 'good cause', many are here because the Daily Worker Bazaar has a justified reputation for selling high quality, often home made goods at affordable prices. Amounts charged in no way reflect the time, effort and materials put into making the sale items. The pricing committee knows working-class people aren't able to pay more, particularly before Christmas. The Bazaar's not operating in a market economy.

At this point I begin to get nervous. My Father's to officially open the bazaar so I look for a suitable place to become more or less invisible. Opening's informal, Father standing relaxed in front of the stage, not on it. He shows the front pages of two national newspapers, the *Daily Worker* and the *Daily Mail*. One of them has a headline in support of a docker's strike, now in its second week. The other berates the Labour Government for continuing its programme of nationalisation. Father uses these diametrically opposed headlines to illustrate the essential need for the *Daily Worker* to ensure voices of working men and women are heard. A murmur of approval diffuses through the audience as 'Ere, Ere' echoes round the room.

I look forward to the Bazaar since it's a chance to buy Christmas presents for my family at knock-down prices, which are even more gratefully received having come from the Bazaar. However, the main reason for my excitement is that many of my aunts and uncles are here

A Political Primer

and I can expect to receive Christmas presents from most of them, usually in cash. Aunty Mary's near one of the stalls and I drift nonchalantly in her direction. Sure enough she greets me with a big smile and a hug, slipping two half-crowns into my hand. That's a good start. Next, Uncle Jim comes into my line of vision. Frowned upon by Mother, but very generous, he comes over to me, Capstan Full Strength cigarette dangling from his mouth. Through the smoke haze he hands me paper money; a ten shilling note. This is the most I've ever been given and I quickly hide it in my shirt pocket. If Mother sees the note she'll think it far too much and insist it's given back. With successful concealment, I look forward to spending the windfall at a later date. Aunty Bessie's also there but, as one of the more conscientious and committed Party members, she's too busy on the stall for me to approach. I'll catch up with her later.

The day goes swimmingly. Most of the goods have been sold and a large sum of money raised for the *Daily Worker*. I've bought three second hand books: *Call of the Wild* by Jack London, *The Water Babies* by Charles Kingsley and *The Secret Seven* by Enid Blyton. The last book's a bit young for me, but having enjoyed *The Famous Five* decide to give it a chance. Two helpings of steaming, nutritious Lancashire hotpot and mushy peas have been consumed, along with several glasses of weak orange cordial. I walk to the bus stop for our journey home with a feeling of deep contentment; and a pocket full of money.

* * *

It's a cold, quiet March morning as I descend the stairs and enter a darkened living room. The curtains are still closed making it difficult to see Mother who's sitting forlornly on the couch looking very sad; in tears. She's reading the *Daily Worker*, and clearly upset. A glance at the newspaper reveals the whole of the front page is given over to a head and shoulders photograph of a man in military uniform, gold braided, red peaked cap. A large moustache partly covers what looks like a faint smile, though steely eyes contradict what might otherwise have been a friendly face. I recognise the face from the *Soviet Weekly* magazine which usually portrays him with children on his knee - Uncle Joe – or watching peasants gaily dancing and singing Russian folk songs. It's the image of Joseph Stalin who has recently died in the Soviet Union, at his home near Moscow. Mother carefully tears off the front page and displays it in our front window. To her, it's the death of a hero who saved the communist revolution and played a crucial part in defeating Hitler and the Nazis.

* * *

There's to be a visit to Colne and other Lancashire towns by the Queen and Prince Phillip. It's 1955, only two years since the Coronation of Elizabeth II and massive publicity is given to the event both in the local newspaper, the *Colne Times*, as well as on radio. There's much excitement at school and round the town, but not in the Kershaw household. My parents are anti-monarchist refusing even to stand for the National Anthem at theatres, cinemas and other events, much to my chagrin. Mother sometimes joins in singing 'Land of Hope and Glory', changing the words to 'Land of Dope and Tory'. The Royal Visit's to include a motorcade along North Valley Road, a short distance away at the bottom of our street. Can I pluck up courage to go and watch the spectacle, even though my parents might not approve? On this occasion I can, dashing down Townley Street just in time to see the open-topped Royal Limousine slowly drive by. Throngs of people line the road, shouting and cheering as the Royal Party passes. I join in; feeling a pang of betrayal.

* * *

Both my parents are atheists, though not fervently so, coming across more as agnostic. In fact my maternal grandmother belongs to the Spiritualist Church and aunts on my Father's side are active in the local Methodists. Hewlett Johnson, Christian Marxist 'Red' Dean of Canterbury, is a family hero: 'If all Christians were like Hewlett Johnson, I might take them more seriously' comments Mother. Her best friend, Marretta, is a committed christian and we often go along to church social events with her. I'm even sent to the local Sunday school, often enjoyable for younger children, singing *'Stand Up, Sit Down for Jesus'* with all the actions, as well as painting and drawing pictures of Bible stories; Baby Jesus in the Cradle,

A Political Primer

Jacob's Coat of Many Colours, David and Goliath.

When a little older, I move to a more formal setting with rows of chairs and a mini-sermon from the Minister. At the end of the sermon there's a collection, but I haven't been made aware of this. The Minister starts to walk along the rows of seated children holding a collection pouch, a cloth bag attached to a short wooden handle. I earnestly observe from my seat near the back, trying to discern whether money's being put in or taken out of the pouch. Though I watch carefully, since children put their hand actually into the bag, it's still unclear. The bag moves closer. I become more and more apprehensive, beginning to blush and sweat. Under pressure as the pouch approaches, I finally decide that, since it's filtered through to me that the Church is 'Good', then the Minister must be giving rather than receiving. That I haven't been provided with money by Mother reinforces this conclusion.

I take money out.

* * *

'Have the newspapers come, Roy?' asks Mother. 'They seem late.'

It's early Monday morning and Mother wants to read the *Daily Worker* before setting off for work at Broughton's cotton mill. I look out of the living room window to see the paperboy dashing up the steps towards our house. He's new. I recognise him from grammar school, though he's a couple of forms ahead of me. The boy, Richard Foulds, lives nearby, but not on our council estate. His father's under-manager with Redmond's grocery chain, so they live in a slightly posher row of private terraced properties, higher up Langroyd Road. They've a front room *and* a living room with large fully fitted kitchen. A small front garden has well-tended rose bushes; bay window. They're strongly Conservative so we don't associate with them, though my brother Len fancies the daughter, Anthea. Nipped in the bud by Mr Foulds.

I pick up the newspapers from behind the front door. The *Daily Herald*, owned and financed by the trade unions; the *Daily Worker*, owned and financed by its readers and the Communist Party; and the Soviet Union. Both papers have large black, sensational headlines.

Russian Tanks crush Hungarian Freedom Fighters
screams the *Daily Herald*.

Russia stops Western led Counter-Revolution in Hungary
explains the *Daily Worker*.

Mother grabs the newspapers, throwing the *Herald* down in disgust whilst avidly reading the *Worker*.

Picking up my satchel, I leave the house to catch the school bus. At the bus stop a number of grammar school pupils are mulling around, including Richard Foulds. He shouts abusively at me.

'Your dad's a Commie. You get the *Daily Worker*. I know because I delivered it this morning.' I try to ignore him, but he continues shouting 'Commie scum, Commie scum.'

There are murmurs of approval by some of the others, but my friends from the council estate tell him to 'Shut up'. We board the bus where I sit alone in embarrassed silence.

At about seven in the evening my Father returns from his trade union office in Manchester. He looks glum.

'I've been talking with Billy Whittaker. He's had a letter from a Hungarian comrade who says the situation's very tense in Budapest. American agents are stoking up demonstrations, but people don't like Russian tanks on their streets. Many young people have been killed and injured.'

'Mr and Mrs Appleton have left the Party' Mother adds. 'Their son Brian's being abused at school and they don't want him to suffer because of their politics. Other Party members might do the same.'

'Yes, it might happen,' agrees Father. 'But quitting the Party won't help. America's been trying to stir up trouble all over Eastern Europe, but they won't win. We'll just have to keep our heads down for a while.'

I go to bed despondent. Everybody seems to be against communists. Every night on the television news there's a barrage of criticism about Hungary .... ; about Russia's atomic bombs ....; about communist led disruptive strikes.

'Propaganda! Propaganda!' Mother shouts at the offending newscaster.

A Political Primer

'Maybe Mum and Dad are actually not communists, but just say they are to show support for the working class and to oppose capitalist bosses' I think, debating with myself; though with little conviction. Tossing and turning in bed, I try to rationalise conflicting emotions: 'Communism's sweeping the world as far as I can see. China's communist as well as the Soviet Union and Eastern European countries. Many freedom movements in colonial countries are led by communists; Malaysia, Kenya, Indonesia, South Africa as well as Cuba. The world atlas is turning Red' I try to convince myself. 'Russia's launched the Sputnik; industrialization is steaming ahead, the *Daily Worker* says so. The Soviet Union and other communist countries win most medals at the Olympics and other sporting events. *Soviet Weekly* reports record harvests on the communal farms. Everybody has plenty to eat; everybody has a job; everybody's equal. Surely communism's a good ideology' I conclude. 'My Dad isn't paid much as a trade union leader. He could earn much more working for Courtaulds, but doesn't because he wants to help exploited working men and women. Mum's worked hard all her life as a weaver, helping her family and others with compassion. No selfishness.'

I read an article in the *Daily Worker*.

'From each according to his ability, to each according to his need'. To me this seems a supremely ethical Mantra. The article continues: *'Such an arrangement will be made possible by the abundance of goods and services that a developed communist society will produce; the idea is that, with full development of socialism and unfettered productive forces, there will be enough to satisfy everyone's needs'.*

'Surely the peak of idealism?' I think to myself.

The following day I go to school determined to stand up to Richard Foulds and refute his allegations, but in the event I don't have to. I'm popular with other pupils, even the older ones. I'm in the school football team, a good swimmer and athlete as well as coming top of the class in the last exams. Pop music's all-encompassing and I'm regarded as one of the coolest, clicking fingers as I stroll along corridors. I even get credit for arguing with teachers about politics. Girls, particularly the younger ones, are attracted to my curly locks, all adding up to a level of kudos way above that of Richard Foulds. He stays quiet.

* * *

'What about Hungarian freedom fighters being crushed by Soviet tanks?' challenges David Wilson, a schoolboy friend.

'What about EOKA freedom fighters in Cyprus or Mau Mau freedom fighters in Kenya?' I respond. 'You call them terrorists, but they're only fighting against oppressive colonial rule. One man's freedom fighter's another man's terrorist.'

'The Russians are exploding bigger and bigger atomic bombs, threatening us all with nuclear annihilation. And now it's the neutron bomb' continues David.

'America has far more atomic weapons than Russia, and has actually used them in Japan' I retort. David's nonplussed.

'Strikes are ruining the country'. David tries again.

'Unions protect living standards of ordinary working people. It's the capitalist bosses causing the problems.'

The maths teacher brings the debate to an end. We move on to quadratic equations.

In fact, David's my best friend. Along with other mates we sometimes have outrageous political arguments in the pub. Since most of the gang are right wing, I'm often in a minority of one but, surprisingly, debates are always good humoured.

'If your dad's a bus conductor, then you should be a bus conductor. The working class should keep in their place' claims Jack in an extravagant exclamation of his political views. We all collapse in laughter at such a ridiculous statement.

'What nonsense, Jack. Just because your dad has a stall in the market selling broken biscuits doesn't make him a successful entrepreneur' I respond.

The beer flows, arguments get increasingly absurd; louder and louder, though it's all done in a jovial, almost hilarious tenor with great bonhomie. After all, we're all teenagers concerned more with sport, pop music, fashion; and girls.

* * *

Mr Land, our English teacher, sets an essay for homework. At first

A Political Primer

I think 'what rubbish', though after more thought, express another view in my essay.

The Best Things in Life are Free

'The amazing English countryside is free, strolling through green meadows in summer and golden, rustling, leaf-laden woods in autumn. Watching fish swim in rippling blue waters of a river. Bird song creating heavenly music. Walking with the one you love, and kissing her by the factory wall, is free. Gazing with wonder at sparkling stars in a clear winter, dark skied canopy, is free. Listening to the New World Symphony, soaring violins, melancholy oboe; or the pounding beat of Rock Around the Clock on a transistor radio, is free. (Almost)

'Up a Lazy River by the old mill stream,
Lazy river in the noon day sun.
Linger awhile in the shade of a tree.
Throw away your troubles, dream with me.

Up a Lazy River where the robin's song,
Wakes the mornin', we roll along.
Make me blue skies above,
Everyone's in love.
Up a Lazy River, how happy we'll be.
Up A Lazy River with me.

Satchmo's right. The best things in life **are** free!

But the miner working hundreds of feet underground all week, coming home too tired to do much more than sleep, doesn't enjoy such 'freedoms'. Neither can my mother, slaving for 45 hours a week in a hot, humid weaving shed before coming home to cook, wash, clean and look after boisterous kids.

Meanwhile, Lord Muck's punting on the Thames before picnicking on the river bank, huge wicker hamper full of cucumber sandwiches, caviar and other delicacies, all swilled down with Mum Cordon Rouge Brut Champagne.

The Best Things in Life are F£ree – if you can afford to experience them!'

We study two books in Mr Land's class: *Oliver Twist* by Charles Dickens and *Les Miserables* by Victor Hugo. In my eyes, both profoundly illustrate the unfairness and inequality of capitalist society. Unusually, I speak up in class.

'Oliver comes out alright in the end, but for every Oliver there are a hundred starving urchins.'

'The guilty one is not he who commits the sin, but the real sinner is he who causes the darkness'. I quote from *Les Miserables* adapting the quote: 'Poverty's not caused by the poor but by the unequal capitalist system.'

The class isn't convinced – nor Mr Land.

* * *

'Here's a book I think you'll find interesting.'

Mr Land gives me a copy of *'Animal Farm'* by George Orwell. I'm suspicious since I know my parents regard Orwell as a traitor to the socialist cause, even though he professes to be a democratic socialist himself. Orwell's support for the International Brigade in Spain isn't enough to bring him back into the fold. Nevertheless I read the book, though with some pain. It filters through that there may be some truth in what Orwell writes, even though it's sub-titled *'A Fairy Story'*.

The pain reminds me of watching a play on BBC television with my parents some years before; an adaptation of another George Orwell book *'1984'*. The play vividly portrays an authoritarian state with omnipresent government surveillance; oppressive rule in the name of a supposed greater good. 'Big Brother is watching you' is a constant theme. *'Thoughtcrimes'* are punished in Room 101, a torture chamber

A Political Primer

in the *'Ministry of Love'* in which the Party attempts to subject a prisoner to his own worst phobias.

'Turn that rubbish off' Mother shouts, though we continue to watch. 'Absolutely biased propaganda' Father scornfully comments. 'This isn't what a communist society would be like. What nonsense. Communism puts power into the hands of the people.'

I'm too young to fully understand the play or my parents' response, but painful feelings of isolation persist.

CHAPTER 2

Travels with My Mother

It's Sunday morning. Mother and I are waiting to board the Ribble bus at Colne bus station to take us over White Moor to Barnoldswick. This is a regular trip to visit my maternal grandparents Ellen and Jud, Aunty Clarice, Uncle Jim and three cousins.

'Can't we go on the other bus, Mum?' I plead.

It's claustrophobic on the Ribble, travelling along narrow, winding roads; up and down, up and down, following the contours of the moorland landscape. Like being on a rolling sea or a retarded fairground waltzer. I'm always travel sick.

'No we can't, Mother replies, 'there isn't a bus for another hour, and anyway it takes a lot longer going through Kelbrook and Salterforth instead of over the Moor. Here, eat an apple, it'll settle your stomach.' It doesn't. I feel nauseous for the whole journey and it's with great relief when we alight in Barlick.

The main street has a number of elegant Victorian houses, many of them with original sagging tiled roofs and wooden Georgian window frames. But what could have been a picturesque scene is spoilt by brash new shops, windows cluttered with garish posters: 'Things go better with Coca Cola'; 'Omo adds brightness to whiteness'; 'Smooth duMaurier cigarettes'; 'Butlins for your holiday'; 'Rowntree's fruitgums – taste the fruit'. Alma Cogan's on stage at Skipton Empire; 'Not to be Missed' shouts the hoarding. Outside the cinema, posters advertise 'Attack of the 50ft Woman', a film I'd like to see, but know I won't be given the chance. Across the street's the sixteenth century Church of St Mary le Ghyll, bells ringing and parishioners, in their Sunday best, trickling through the ornate, ancient, stone-gated entrance.

It's an overcast, dismal day and flurries of drizzle force us to take shelter in shop doorways. As we reach level crossings near the railway

Travels with My Mother

station, the gates close and the piercing whistle of a steam train makes me jump. Steam gushes out of the engine almost enveloping the scene with a damp swirling cloud. I rush to the gate to see if I can catch the number of the train. Maybe it's a 'Namer' which I'll be able to add to my train spotting record book? But I'm out of luck. It isn't a 'Namer' and I don't even manage to see the full number. Maybe I'll make one up.

As we hurry towards Grandma's house, the surroundings change, with cobbled streets narrowing and a wet mist rising from glistening pavements. Long rows of back-to-backs seem to block out what little light there is. Walking down Jubilee Street, avoiding stray dogs rummaging in the gutters, we eventually arrive. Mother pushes open the rattling gate and we enter what would normally be the back yard; but since the houses are back-to-back, this is also the front entrance. Mother opens the door without knocking.

'Mother, are you there?'

No response, so we walk through the kitchen, not much more than a scullery, into the main room which acts as front room, dining room and lounge all in one. Grandma Ellen's dozing on the well-worn sofa. The fire's gone out in the big, black, metalled range which covers most of one wall.

'Mother. Why are you sitting in the dark; and with the fire out? You'll catch your death.' Grandma Ellen wakes with a start.

'What did you say?' She asks drowsily.

'I said why is it dark, and why isn't there a fire?' Mother repeats.

'We've no more mantles for the gaslight and no matches to light the fire' comes an irritated reply.

Mother goes into the kitchen and rummages about in the cupboards and shelves eventually finding both mantles and matches. Within a few minutes the gas lights are lit and a fire begins to warm the room; and Grandma. Mother puts on the kettle to make tea and settles down in the only easy chair whilst I sit on a stool in the corner. Little is said; we're a taciturn family.

'Roy's passed his eleven-plus' Mother proudly announces. Grandma doesn't respond.

'The Co-op ran out of butter last week; we had to have marg' Grandma complains grumpily. 'What's your Harry doing about it?' She knows my dad's President of Colne Co-op, but doesn't understand that he has nothing to do with stock levels in Barlick. 'Too much milk in this tea, Martha.'

After a few minutes, Grandfather Jud comes in. Despite the cold, damp weather he wears only a long sleeved striped, granddad collar shirt, sleeves rolled up to the elbows, baggy trousers held up with a piece of cord. Scrawny forearms are white and hairy; hands rough and calloused from years of oiling and repairing looms in the nearby weaving shed. He does little more than acknowledge our presence with a jerky nod of his cloth-capped head.

'Ellen, we're a' them chips I left on't range last neet? The' wer' a lot left'

'They're in't oven if ye look, but lord knows why ye want to keep 'em; all cold and greasy.'

'Waste not, want not' he explains.

By now I need the toilet, not only for a wee, but also for a 'number two'. Minimal toilet facilities are in the yard. It's dark with no light, either electric or gas and the toilet doesn't flush; just a plank of wood with two large holes drilled out leading directly to the distant sewer below. I know it's distant because of the time it takes to hear the 'plop'. No toilet roll, only sheets of rough newspaper cut into small squares; neither comfortable nor effective. Despite the urgency, I decide to hold on until we reach Uncle Jim's.

* * *

Jim and Clarice live in a row of houses on Railway Terrace, the railway line running on the opposite side of the street. This house isn't back-to-back and has a small garden at the front, as well as a back yard. We push our way through the gate to find Cousin Frank tinkering with his moped. It's all in bits, as it always seems to be when we visit. 'Don't think I've ever seen him riding it' I think to myself. Frank doesn't notice our arrival as he tries to replace a spark plug, bare arms covered in oil and grease. Everyone to his own.

Gales of laughter emanate from the well-lit front room, since there's electricity in this part of town. Half-closed curtains reveal a scene of uninhibited mirth as Uncle Jim holds forth with dodgy tales of dodgy deals. An unexpected visitor is sitting in an armchair near a cosy, crackling fire, rolling from side to side with uncontrolled glee.

Travels with My Mother

It's another cousin, Clarice, who's been brought over to Barlick by Uncle Harold in his Morris Minor car. Clarice is severely handicapped with a form of Parkinson's disease, unable to control her muscles, breathing or swallowing. But this doesn't stop her joining in with the hilarity of Jim's stories. Her laughter's infectious and her namesake, Aunty Clarice, has tears of joy running down her face. I dash across the room to the stairs leading to the upstairs toilet. The stairs are steep, narrow, and difficult to negotiate, my ascent being made even more difficult by boxes of red tar soap, as well as bottles of disinfectant and bleach. It smells like a hospital or school, the latter explaining the stock of cleaning materials. Jim's just started a job as school caretaker and there always seem to be 'perks' with each new job.

Coming back down the stairs, I hear music drifting up from the living room. A record of *The Kerry Dance* is being played on an old fashioned gramophone, steel needle scratching the 78 r.p.m record as the turntable spins; though the sound's no less cheerful. It's Cousin Clarice's favourite song and the whole family joins in, Jim performing all the actions, playing invisible instruments.

'We danced to the band with the curious tone
Of cornet, clarinet and big trombone
Fiddle, 'cello, big bass drum
Bassoon, flute and euphonium
Each one making the most of his chance
Altogether in the Floral Dance.'

Clarice joins in, arms flinging out in time to the music, face contorted with joy as she tries to sing the well-loved words. Her ebullience lights up the room.

Sadly, this is the last time I am to see Cousin Clarice. A few months later she dies, unable to swallow, choking on an apple she's not supposed to eat.

* * *

We arrive at a scrap yard in Barlick, having eventually found it round behind the gasworks. Uncle Jim's in a corner of the yard, wearing greasy, stained overalls; saw and screwdriver in hand. He's looking at, what appears to me, a pile of scrap metal and wood.

'Martha, here's the caravan I told you about' Jim announces. 'It needs a lot of work doing to it, but I can promise you a smashing holiday home by the time I've finished.'

Looking at the twisted mass, I have grave doubts. The pile of scrap is, in fact, the carcass of a caravan Jim has found (we don't ask where). Mother and two of her sisters, Clarice and Mary, have joined forces to pay for the caravan and its restoration. They've every confidence in Jim since he's performed DIY miracles in the past and have no doubts he can do it again.

Jim's the loveable rogue of the family. A heavy smoker, Capstan Full Strength, and a moderate drinker, the sisters had been impressed with his uninhibited life style and raucous sense of humour. He's also been in the Royal Marines, adding to the appeal. Mother hadn't approved but was swept along by sisterly solidarity though this was tested to the full when Jim got a job with Barnoldswick Co-operative Society as a coal wagon driver. Most people have coal fires, and sacks of coal are delivered weekly from a central coal yard. At first Mother approves; after all, he's working for the Co-op, but later it comes out that after completing his Co-op round, Jim would go back to the yard, load the wagon up again with sacks of coal to be delivered to his own private customers. Family relationships are strained for some time.

Three months later the caravan's complete. Jim has lived up to his word, multifarious practical skills having produced a splendid 4-birth holiday home with top quality workmanship and materials. All Jim's faults are forgiven despite the dubiousness of material sources. Not only that, Jim's found a perfect site for the caravan at Red Bank Farm in Bolton-le-Sands, near Morecambe.

A long standing tradition in Lancashire cotton towns is the Wakes Week holiday. Most cotton workers and their families go to the coast for these well-earned breaks, usually Blackpool or Morecambe, depending to some extent on the strata of society a family considers itself to occupy. Almost everybody's working class, but some are more working class than others. Blackpool attracts the brasher fun-loving, often younger holiday makers, ready for a beer, fish and chips and a kiss-me-quick hat. Morecambe's more refined with an older clientele, likely to stroll along the prom or listen to a brass band in Happy Mount Park. My Mother's family are 'Morecambe' working class (a little bit superior and certainly not vulgar). The caravan site's small and exclusive, in a field overlooking the shore and Morecambe Bay. No large, regimented caravan site for our family.

* * *

This is the earliest I've ever been up in the morning; five o'clock and still dark. Mother and I are setting off for a holiday in London, my first visit to the Capital. Father's risen even earlier to make breakfast and the appetising aroma of bacon and eggs suffuses the air; the smell of excitement; the taste of excitement. Toast made from a farmhouse loaf, spread with Co-op Avondale butter (no Stork margarine in this household). Fresh real coffee, not instant, with Channel Island milk to be added. It's a mile and a half walk to Colne Railway Station. We don't have a car, there's no bus service so early in the morning and Mother won't pay for a taxi on principle. So we walk, carrying two suitcases. At the station, Mother buys comics for me to read on the train, *Film Fun* and *Tiger*, thought to be more educational than American Marvel comics.

The huge train arrives at the station, coming to a halt in clouds of steam billowing from all parts of the engine. Suddenly there's an ear piercing scream as high pressure steam's released from the hard working engine. We all jump, startled by the sudden shrill noise. The train's on time and we're helped in boarding by the station master, who is a communist friend of my Father. He's dressed in a smart, navy blue serge suit, white shirt, dark blue tie and waistcoat with gold-coloured chains holding whistle and pocket watch. A British Railway emblem on the tie is repeated on the badge fastened to the front of a nebbed, military looking cap. It's not a corridor train and there aren't many passengers, so we have a compartment to ourselves.

Mother struggles to lift our suitcases onto the string-netted overhead rack. Framed pictures of trains and country scenes adorn the compartment interior above the long upholstered bench seats, which I inspect closely. Pictures of the Royal Scot and Mallard record the achievements of British Rail at its best. Watercolour prints show the English countryside in all its glory with thatched cottages nestling on the bank of a meandering river and black and white Friesian cattle gently grazing in hawthorn-hedged green fields. Scythed haymakers follow the horse drawn wagon. 'Makes me proud to be British' I think to myself.

The Stationmaster blows his whistle, but this is drowned out by the booming sound of the engine's 'steam trumpet'. Clanging sounds come from huge iron engine wheels, bigger than me, as they begin to turn, clouds of steam blotting out views of the departing station. The compartment's musty with stale air so Mother opens the window, using a leather strap on the door. The window crashes down with a thud allowing steam and soot laden smoke to pour into the carriage. She grabs the strap again to try and close the window, but it's more difficult to close than it was to open. Nevertheless, she finally manages the task, slumping down onto the seat with a sigh. 'We're going to London. We're going to London' I chant to the rhythm of the train.

We arrive at Paddington Station, opening the carriage door to a tumultuous noise. Passengers and tourists are rushing everywhere, walking with a purpose. Men in bowler hats and striped suits, holding umbrellas like swords, striding resolutely towards waiting limousines. Young women dressed in the latest fashions, inelegantly push their way through the turnstiles. Smartly uniformed schoolchildren carry well laden satchels. Porters tout for business, pushing trolleys loaded with expensive suitcases. Newspaper sellers shout out the headlines: 'Prostitute murdered in Hackney'; 'Gnomes of Zurich arrive in London'. It's even busier outside the station as black London cabs jostle for fares in the taxi ranks and long queues of passengers at the bus stop argue as they board. A police car and ambulance, blue lights flashing and sirens blaring, edge their way through the congested traffic. So this is London!

I'm intimidated by the scene, but not so Mother. She spots a policeman. 'Looks just like Dixon of Dock Green, smart but crumpled uniform, helmet at a slight angle' I observe. With bravado, Mother walks up to him.

'Excuse me constable, can you tell me where to catch the number 32 bus. I want to get to Liberty Street.'

This is where our bed & breakfast boarding house is located. Mother had found the guesthouse in the Daily Worker small ads section, so we can expect a friendly welcome.

'Yes, madam. The bus stop's over there on the corner next to the café'

Travels with My Mother

the friendly, helpful 'Bobby' replies. 'Hope you have an enjoyable stay in London.'

We certainly do. Every morning, after an early breakfast, we leave the boarding house to walk, walk, and walk again the streets of the City. Sometimes we use the Tube, a whoosh of warm air surrounding the moving staircase as we go down, down to the underground, joining the crush of passengers trying to board overloaded trains. But mainly we walk. The Tower of London with its Beefeaters and Ravens; Madam Tussauds, including the Chamber of Horrors with a glowering, fist clenched Adolf Hitler (I'm not scared, only fascinated). I imagine the screams of a rogue on the rack as he's stretched from five feet to six feet. Into Oxford Circus, though no clowns or animals; no horses with tutu wearing balancing girls. We see the Houses of Parliament with towering Big Ben reaching to the sky, pounding out the chimes I've heard every morning on our radio before the BBC News. Briefly to Buckingham Palace (no homage paid here); Horse Guards Parade (how do the soldiers keep so still?); a short boat ride on the magnificent Thames; The Natural History Museum, full of the wonders of the world. Mother drags me to the 'Piltdown Man' exhibition. 'This is the missing link between humans and apes' she explains. Returning each evening to the guesthouse, we're tired and sweaty from our exertions in the dusty, damp London air, but full of wonder and elation.

One day we visit the Daily Worker Offices on Farringdon Road. Enthusiastically welcomed by one of the reporters, we're shown round the news room; a bustling, cigarette smoke filled office with earnest, wooly-jumpered journalists speaking on the many phones, typing on the many typewriters. Photographs of well-known communists line the wall with Lenin taking prominence. We go into the editor's room, but he's too busy to talk to us. Mother gives the secretary a large, white £5 note (I've never seen one before).

'This is for the Daily Worker Fighting Fund' explains Mother, proud of her contribution to the 'Cause'.

Further down the road is London Co-operative Society's Café and, as it's lunchtime, we go in. It's genteel; wooden Victorian chairs and tables; prim waitresses wearing neat black dresses, white aprons and bonnets. I examine the ornate menu.

'I want 'Welsh Rabbit', Mum' I request, politely. But when the dish arrives, it appears to be cheese on toast.

'I asked for rabbit' I grumble. Mother laughs and explains, but I'm not happy until the second course arrives – my first Knickerbocker Glory. 'Welsh Rabbit' no longer has much appeal.

* * *

We arrive in Princes Street in the evening, the journey from Colne having been long and tedious, with many toilet stops. Mother and I alight from the coach onto a wide flagged pavement, once again clutching our suitcases. The street scene's bustling with rushing, hunched figures; like a Lowry painting except the figures are dressed in quality, fashionable clothes rather than flat caps and cheap suits. As well as ornate street lamps, strings of coloured lights stretch down the boulevard, like Christmas decorations though it's only early October. High windowed shop fronts are dazzlingly lit, displaying sumptuous goods for sale. Jenners Emporium has elegant mannequin dummies draped in the latest Paris fashions, further adorned with plaid scarves. A rugged looking male mannequin wears a tartan kilt; Clan Campbell Kilt informs a small, tastefully designed, copperplate sign. I look for price tags, but there are none. 'The Whisky Shop' window has rows and rows of artistically shaped bottles displayed on tartan cloth-covered shelves. 'Lagavulin, 16 year old malt'; 'The Glenrothes'; 'Highland Park'. The range of whiskies seems endless. 'Why would people want so many different whiskies?' I ask myself. 'How greedy.' The adjacent shop has dimpled glass Georgian style bay windows advertising 'Authentic Scottish Delicacies'. Highland Shortbread; Oatcakes; Arbroath Smokie; Black Puddings; and Haggis. Except for the Shortbread, nothing sounds palatable to me.

A black, shiny Austin A40 car pulls up at the kerbside and out jumps a young woman wearing a warm looking, dark olive wool coat, as well as tartan scarf and beret.

'Martha, glad you've made it. Sorry we're late, the traffic down Princes Street is impossible at this time.'

'Ethel, nice to see you again. We've only just arrived' Mother replies with the tiniest of white lies.

Travels with My Mother

'This must be your son, Roy' Ethel warmly says, looking at me with welcoming eyes. She moves towards me so I retreat, but can't escape the enthusiastic hug and kiss. 'He's a handsome boy.' I blush, eyes glued to the pavement. 'John's driving the car. We better get in quickly before a policeman books us for parking.' John puts the suitcases in the ample boot and we jump in the back seat.

Ethel and her husband John are communist friends of my Mother and Father. They'd met on a demonstration in London against nuclear weapons. On the coach journey up to Edinburgh Mother had told me that, as well as being communists, the McKenzie's were also Quakers. 'I'm not religious but Quakers seem to share many of our ideals, so I'm happy to join with them' explains Mother. 'I went to one of their Meetings last time I was in Edinburgh. Everyone sat in a big circle. Nobody spoke for a long time; complete silence. Then a young woman in shawl and bonnet stood up and asked God to bring Peace to the World. It was quite moving.'

We arrive at their apartment near the city centre, which is quite plush. With this and the car, the McKenzie's seem well-to-do, unlike most of Mother's communist friends. 'John's a lecturer at Edinburgh University' Mother tells me, almost apologetically.

The next morning, Mr McKenzie drops us off at the entrance to Princes Street Gardens. It's thronged with people, despite the inclement weather. 'There's the Scott Monument' Mother enthusiastically informs me. Sir Walter Scott's one of her favourite authors, tattered copies of *Rob Roy*, *Ivanhoe* and *Kenilworth* often to be found on our sideboard. To my relief, Mother decides not to climb the 287 steps inside the monument. I know there's going to be a lot of walking today; there always is. Ambling along the tree lined avenue, I catch glimpses of Edinburgh Castle. 'This is a *real* castle' I think to myself. The high stone walls seem to have been hewn out of the rocky cliff face itself while towers and ramparts speak of a turbulent military history. I gird my loins in anticipation of the hard trek up to the Castle and we're soon climbing up the long, steep steps leading to Edinburgh old town. Granite buildings breathe history and memories of stoic heroes of Scottish folklore, as does the Castle.

Our walking tour of Scottish history doesn't end there. After a brief stop for lunch (Mother insists we have haggis with neeps and tatties, surprisingly eatable), we set off for Calton Hill. Again this involves walking up a steep path with wide stone steps worn thin by centuries of visitors. At the summit, even Mother has to sit down for a rest, out of breath with the day's exertions; but we don't sit for long. Mother has come to see the Robert Burns Monument and give homage to her best-loved working-class poet. I'm impressed, but not as much as with a colossal monument which looks as though it's been transplanted from ancient Greece. With difficulty I climb up the huge blocks of granite towards the Parthenon style Doric Columns. Leaning against one of the huge columns, my arm hugging the cold, fluted stone pillar, I marvel at the panorama before me. In the distance are the 'banks and braes' surrounding Edinburgh. The Castle and Arthur's Seat can be clearly seen, trying to glisten in the pale sunlight that's broken through a cloudy sky. Other monuments on Calton Hill seem to crowd in around me. Robert Burns; Dugald Stewart; Political Martyrs.

The view that rivets my attention most is of Princes Street, The Royal Mile. Cars, trams and buses weave their way up and down the wide, tree-lined boulevard. The wide pavement's crowded as shoppers, businessmen, hawkers and street cleaners mingle, much more politely than in London. Solid stone buildings have retained their Georgian elegance and ornate monuments add to the atmosphere of a capital city content with its turbulent history and place in the world. I gaze at the scene with a kind of reverence.

'Roy, come on down; be careful' shouts Mother. 'We have to catch the coach back to Colne this evening.'

I climb down the granite base, managing to scrape my knee on a projecting ledge. I'm not looking forward to the journey home, but my first experience of Scotland has been magical.

* * *

Having been to London and Edinburgh our next visit, to Wales, seems a bit of an afterthought. This trip's not to Cardiff but to Llangollen in the Welsh valleys.

'We're going to Llangollen on Sunday, Roy' Mother informs me. 'It's only for the day but I want to see where they hold the Eisteddfod.' My family love Welsh male voices and we frequently play a record of the Treorchy Choir. But there's no chance of hearing a Choir, or any other musical performances, on our short trip.

Travels with My Mother

Reasons for going to Llangollen are partly political, because of its connection with Paul Robeson, the Black American bass singer. Paul Robeson's another family hero who, as a communist sympathiser, was harassed by the American Government and had his passport taken away. Despite this, he'd managed to make contact with Welsh miners, supporting their struggle against the 'mine bosses'. He'd also addressed the Miners Eisteddfod in 1957 via a transatlantic link. Our trip is, in fact, a pilgrimage to Welsh choirs, the Eisteddfod, miners - and Paul Robeson.

We manage to get a front seat on the coach, giving us a panoramic view of the Welsh countryside. It doesn't have the grandeur of Scotland, but nevertheless has a rolling beauty with stonewalled, moss green farm fields looking peaceful in bright sunlight. Sparsely wooded hills are a darker green with brown rocky outcrops and sheep foraging in the sparser pastures. From time to time slate quarries interrupt the landscape, as do occasional mining slag heaps. We pass through small villages, not much more than hamlets, with quaint, beautifully preserved cottages, the sound of church bells often adding to picturesque scenes.

Compared with London and Edinburgh, Llangollen is a haven of peace. We walk on the banks of the River Dee and visit the railway station to watch a small antiquated engine puffing along. Canal boats lazily cross the aqueduct, boat owners waving contentedly at passers-by. We manage to find the International Eisteddfod Pavilion, in the entrance hall of which are many photographs of past performers. Ukrainian and Estonian folk groups and musicians and singers from other east European countries; but mainly Welsh performers in red coats, tall black hats and shawls. But no pictures of Paul Robeson.

* * *

Mother and I again alight from a coach, this time at the bus station in Morecambe. We've had a long journey, by bus to Burnley changing to the long distance service to the Lancashire coastal town. We're weighed down with a suitcase and other luggage, struggling to reach yet another bus stop to catch a double-decker; destination Bolton-le-Sands, though this is not the end of our journey. From the bus stop, we now have a walk of over a mile along Pasture Lane before joining the coastal path to Red Bank Farm. I look pleadingly at the one or two cars that pass us, but none of them stop to give us a lift, so we continue to trudge along the seemingly endless lane.

We arrive at the caravan exhausted, though our exertions don't end there. I have to bring water from the farmyard in a large, white enamel bucket. When filled to the brim, the bucket's too heavy for me to carry, so three quarters full has to do. Even then, water spills out as I clumsily struggle to bring the pail back to the caravan. Next task is to clean out the chemical toilet drum which, though empty, needs to be rinsed at the farmyard tap and disinfectant added. Empty, this is no problem, but later in the week the receptacle, now full of smelly urine and solid matter, will have to be emptied. 'Ugh!' Finally the gas cylinder proves to be empty so I have to go to the farmhouse to buy a replacement, again quite heavy. Oh, the joys of camping!

The next day we set off early to walk to Carnforth railway station, a long walk though pleasant in spring sunshine. As we amble along the sea front, seagulls and curlews dive, screaming at us not to disturb their hidden nests. The country lane leading to Carnforth is narrow and winding with cottages, brightly painted in pink, yellow and other pastel shades, having big gardens, enclosed by low dry stone walls. Gardens are well tended, full of roses, dahlias, irises and other English favourites; crimson, blue/violet, pink, white, and yellow. Most of the properties are owned by retired well-to-do couples with plenty of time to devote to their horticultural hobby. Gardens to be proud of.

Arriving early at the station, Mother buys tickets for our journey to Barrow-in-Furnace before we go to the refreshment room for a cup of tea and a toasted teacake. 'This tea room's famous. It's where the film Brief Encounter was made' Mother confides. 'Celia Johnson and Trevor Howard were the stars.' Mother keeps her eye on the station clock, also famous for being in the film, to make sure we don't miss the train.

'The 10.45 train for Barrow-in-Furnace is now arriving at platform 2' announces a muffled voice over the platform speakers. 'Will passengers please board immediately as the train is scheduled to depart in just two minutes.' We quickly climb on board, but Mother realises we're in a 1st class carriage, so we equally quickly get off again and walk down the platform to the 'proletariat' part of the train, as she calls

Travels with My Mother

it. We reboard just in time as the stationmaster waves his flag and blows his authoritative whistle as the huge wheels turn, and steam and soot fill the air. We're off.

The journey round Morecambe Bay is spectacular, glimpses of sea and shore alternating with scenes of wooded copses and small hamlets. In the Lune estuary small fishing boats are anchored and distant mud flats can be seen protecting active cockle beds. The picturesque village of Grange-Over-Sands and its harbour shimmer in the sunshine. As we steam into Barrow, huge docks and ship-building cranes and equipment come into sight. Alighting at the noisy railway station, instead of going into town we make our way to the adjacent bus station. 'Buses for Walney Island' is displayed on an overhead notice board. We dash to the indicated stop, just managing to scramble on board as the bus pulls out. Walney Island's narrow and windswept with sand dunes giving way to sand, shingle and large pebbles, stretching down to the Irish Sea. Powerful waves pound the shore and the distant horizon speaks of far away, exotic lands. I stand transfixed, filled with a sense of longing to see the world.

* * *

It's a sunny though breezy day at Red Bank Farm caravan site as Mother and I get ready to travel to Morecambe. I pack my 'swimmers' and a towel, the intention being to go to the famous Lido. Instead of walking down the long lane to the bus stop we take a short cut through the field over the top of Red Bank. Sheep graze leisurely, their continual bleats merging with sound of the wind blowing in from the Bay. Gulls dive, their cries and squawks sound menacing as they swoop towards us. The smell of muck-spreading from an adjacent field overpowers the sweet fragrance of fresh grass, buttercups and daisies. Black and white cattle have previously been kept in the field, so I have to skip and jump to avoid treading in the cow claps. Newly purchased, open-toed sandals, worn with short cotton socks, mustn't be sullied if I'm to avoid chastisement. 'Don't let those new sandals get dirty. They cost a fortune' warns Mother.

Views over Morecambe Bay are exhilarating. The rust red of the steep bank contrasts with pale green saltmarsh grass interspersed with dozens of seawater pools reflecting clear blue skies. Beyond the saltmarsh, the wide expanse of mudflats and sandflats vary in hue from light brown, dry sand to the ominously darker quicksands. Grange-Over-Sands can be seen clearly across the bay, shimmering white dots of bungalows sparkling on the hillside. The whole scene's framed by the distant panorama of Lakeland hills and mountains. All's right with the world; for now!

We alight from the bus onto the promenade when the first come-down from my high spirits happens, almost immediately. Mother guides me over to a seaside stall selling shrimps, cockles and mussels and other fresh seafoods. Succulent Morecambe Bay shrimps are famous for their quality and salty freshness. I love them. My mouth waters in anticipation of such a tasty treat. But when we reach the stall, instead of a coned paper bag with pink shrimps peeping out waiting to be beheaded, topped and tailed before eating, I'm presented with a large shell containing what looks like the slimy entrails of a revolting sea creature.

'Eat it up' instructs Mother in her most authoritative voice, 'it's full of iron and vitamins. It's good for you.'

Why is it, I ask myself, that only the most obnoxious foods are 'good for you'. Why does the stale crust of a sliced loaf 'make your hair curl'? (In any case, I hate my curls). Why does uneatable smoked Finnan Haddock increase your brainpower? Why do raw carrots make you see better at night? Most of all, why is stewed, seaweed-like, green spring cabbage a virtual elixir of life? I believe none of it! It's all a ploy to get rid of all the foods that nobody else wants.

Mother forces the shell to my lips and I can't help but let the oyster slide into my unwelcoming mouth. You can make a young boy take an oyster to his mouth, but you can't make him swallow. I'm a polite child and usually do what I'm told; but I can also be stubborn. I refuse to swallow the slimy oyster despite all my Mother's cajoling and parental wiles. We continue to walk along the prom but, nearing the swimming pool, Mother relents. I'm allowed to spit out the offending sea creature, though over the railings onto the pebbled beach, not on the promenade.

I arrive at the swimming pool with some trepidation. It's not a 25 yard pool like the one back home in Colne where I'd been taught to swim by my brother Len. No, this is a huge Stadium with an Olympic size pool and three tiers of diving boards stretching into the clear blue sky. Boys are jumping and diving from the top board, shouting at the

Travels with My Mother

tops of their voices, enjoying the excitement. This is something I'd love to do, but my cautious temperament prevents it. The enormous pool's overlooked by rows and rows of seats on three sides, the whole stadium being open to the elements – no roof. Outside the stadium are huge posters advertising the 'Miss Great Britain Beauty Pageant.' Beautiful young women in one-piece bathing suits (no bikinis in those days) peer out from the posters. Sexual urges not yet having developed, the pictures of bathing beauties do not awaken me; though one long-legged blonde specimen does seem attractive (this particular vision of beauty is to be my 'downfall' in later life). The final of this national competition, much despised by militant feminists, is to be held in a few weeks time at the Stadium. On smaller posters is advertised a 'Bonny Baby Competition', this time not national, but just for local mothers and their adored offspring. Yet another poster near the entrance is prominent, informing passers-by:

TODAY! – BONNY CHILD COMPETITION
BRING YOUR SON OR DAUGHTER ALONG
WIN FABULOUS PRIZES!

Too late! I cotton on that I'm not here to swim but to be embarrassed beyond belief by participating in an excruciating walk around the pool in front of not only the judges but a scattering of parents and the general public. Realisation dawns on me that the reason for Mother relenting on the oyster episode is so she can insist I take part in this tormenting competition. There's no way out. The entrance fee's been paid and I've changed into my dull, black, knitted wool 'cozzie'. Most of the other children are older than me and wear colourful swimming costumes. Many have attractive tans compared with my pasty white, pigeon-chested body. Ambling round the pool disconsolately, I look down at my feet, adopting the best frown I can muster. Surely it will all be over soon when I'm eliminated in the first round?

But, No. The judges call me into the final group of ten to parade again along the poolside. I continue to frown, but to no avail as I'm given second place. The only reason for this success is my blond, curly 'Little Lord Fauntleroy' ringlets. There can be no other explanation. I have to go up to the rostrum for presentation of my 'FABULOUS PRIZE' by Thora Hird who, though unknown to me, is a celebrity actress and comedienne. Mother's impressed and confides in me that Thora's daughter is even more famous; actress Jeannette Scott. Thora's presenting the prizes because she was born in Morecambe where her father was theatre manager and impresario.

'What is this 'FABULOUS PRIZE'?' I ask myself. Having been through nearly two hours of torture, something spectacular's expected, but once again I'm brought back down to earth. There before me is a three-wheeler tricycle; large, but still a tricycle. Wouldn't any child be thrilled with this? Not me! I already have a new, small two-wheeler bike at home so why would I want to go back to three wheels? Nevertheless I make the best of a bad job, jump on the tricycle and head down the promenade. What happened next is lost in the mist of time. All I know is that the tricycle never reached Colne, or even the caravan.

* * *

On the last day of our holiday, Jim, Clarice and my two cousins, Frank and Jean arrive to take over the caravan. Not for Jim long bus journeys and walks to reach the site. He's somehow acquired a Ford Prefect, old, but in full working order. As with most of Jim's deals nobody knows where the car's come from or how he's managed to buy it. Closer inspection however reveals that it's not actually in full working order as tyres are threadbare, the passenger door doesn't open, the mechanical direction indicator doesn't work and the engine squeals. Nevertheless it has transported a family of four and all their luggage the forty or so miles from Barlick to Morecambe. You can't ask for more than that.

Frank's first to emerge from the vehicle, springing out through the passenger window. He's dressed in a short-sleeved Hawaiian shirt, Bermuda shorts and flip flops.

'Roy, let's go down to the shore' he shouts immediately.

I'm not keen since he usually gets me into trouble, but meekly agree. No going round the path and through the farmyard for Frank as he runs

Travels with My Mother

to the low stone wall that surrounds the site and stands astride.

Though the wall's low on the caravan site side, it's much higher where it drops down to the shore. Fearless (or reckless?), Frank lowers himself down the other side onto pebbles below. I take the long way round.

Running across rough saltmarsh grass, Frank inevitably trips and falls into one of the many brackish pools. They're not deep so he's able to pull himself out without difficulty, but his new shirt and shorts are soaked, caked with mud and sand from the pool bed. This antic's become traditional, so no need to worry. Worrying is not one of Frank's 'things'.

BEWARE!
DEEP AND VARYING CHANNELS
QUICKSANDS

The painted wooden notice is planted in the ground on a stake. It's weather worn and at an angle, making it difficult to read, though the message is clear; it's dangerous to go past this point. To Frank this is challenge rather than warning as he runs out onto mud flats, oblivious to danger. I follow, as it's too late to go back now. We wade through one of the channels, but it's only knee-deep so no problem. The mud flats become darker and wetter: 'Maybe this is where quicksand starts' I think, but don't say. Frank sees the concern in my face.

'Don't worry, the tide's still going out so there's no problem with either quicksand or flooded channels.' I'm not convinced.

'Look over there' Frank shouts pointing to what appear to be fishing nets stretched out across several channels. 'They're fishermen's nets in the Lune estuary where they trap salmon and sea trout as fish return to the sea. If we get there before the fishermen, we can take a couple of salmon back with us.'

This sounds like poaching to me so I become very nervous. As we approach the nets I look around. 'What if fishermen come out and catch us? What if we're trapped when the tide comes in?'

'Frank, let's go back' I plead.

'Don't be a scaredycat' he admonishes me, laughing loudly.

Suddenly there's the sound of diesel engines revving up, the noise coming from the shore near Hest Bank where fishing boats are moored. But the tide's out, so there's no chance of boats being launched. Instead, two large vehicles, like small military tanks with caterpillar tracks, are moving out, heading in our direction. Frank's bravado evaporates as he shakes off his flip flops and scampers away at speed with me in his wake. Arriving back at the caravan, out of breath and trembling, Mother's angry when she realizes what's happened. Jim and Frank just laugh. Like father, like son.

CHAPTER 3

Dedicated Follower of Fashion

Pride of place in the small living room of our pebble-dashed council house is given over to Mother's Singer sewing machine. This isn't just a small appliance perched on a table, but a top of the range model integrated into a handsome, dark walnut veneered item of furniture. When not in use, the machine disappears into the body of the furnishing, metamorphosing into a table top displaying favorite ornaments: an ornate Rabbie Burns jug with a quotation – 'The rank is but the guinea's stamp, the Man's the gowd for a'that'; a bust of Karl Marx; a ceramic figurine of a contented looking brown cow; and a cream coloured bowl, full of fresh fruit which we are encouraged to eat 'to clean our teeth and settle our stomachs.' Shiny green Granny Smiths, bright yellow Fyffe's bananas, huge Outspan oranges; and sometimes a bunch of purple grapes.

Below, and connected to the sewing machine is a large wrought iron foot pedal, providing two-footed power at great speed. A plastic cord transports energy from pedal to sewing machine, replaced frequently because of constant use. Each side of the table are two drawers in which cotton reels, scissors, pins, needles, and other sewing accessories reside; but that's not all. The drawers are keepers of much mysterious bric-a-brac with which I'm constantly fascinated. Lead soldiers; badges (bright socialist red); foreign coins from Father's trips abroad; Weaver's Union membership cards; foreign stamps torn from airmail letters; jigsaw puzzle pieces; bone dice; and a small hard back book, beautifully decorated with Islamic designs, of an Omar Khayyam poem: 'The Moving Finger writes; and, having writ, moves on'. I don't understand it, but my imagination's fired by exotic, veiled words.

Mother makes many of her own clothes, and also some for her two sons: shirts, pyjamas; even trousers. But her current project seems more ambitious. Thick, blue, almost royal blue, corduroy material is causing broken needles and unusually dire muttering. After a few evenings, a pair of short trousers appear; my size. I look at them with foreboding. It's another week before the other garment materializes as sewing in the long zip has proved almost impossible; but now it's ready. A tight waisted blouson with raglan sleeves and zip from waist to collar. With the bright, royal blue colour it looks like something worn by the small son of an aristocrat visiting a becastled grandmamma; certainly not to be worn by a working-class boy attending the local junior school.

Next morning I wake to find the newly made outfit on the chair next to my bed. So I'm to wear it for school, Lord Street County Primary School? I search round nervously for my usual grey short trousers, white shirt and navy jumper, but to no avail. I protest to Mother that it doesn't fit and would break school dress rules, again to no avail. I develop a coughing fit, but Mother never falls for that one. All avenues of escape having been blocked, I reluctantly put on the hideous bright blue ensemble, pick up my school bag, and walk slowly down to the bus stop. Maybe I can miss the school bus? No point in that, it would only make matters worse. At first, other pupils pretend not to see me, averting their gaze and talking animatedly to each other. Then Brian Higginbottom arrives, a boy I've recently had a fight with. 'Oh, look at Little Boy Blue' he yells through great peals of laughter. 'Are you going to blow your horn?'

Everyone joins in the ridicule my face turning almost scarlet, contrasting sharply with the blue of my blouson. Embarrassment's complete. Arriving at school, merriment and guffaws continue at my expense. Even the teacher on playground duty can't hide an uncalled for smirk, though there's some relief when my best friend, David, comes over.

'That's a super outfit, wish I had one' he says. Of course it's not true, but since he's leader of a school mini-gang the others tone down their rude comments. 'I'll fight you for it' he continues. We pretend fisticuffs, the other children lose interest and go back to conkers, hopscotch, Chinese burns.

The bell rings for end of the school day. I don't want to venture onto the school bus again, so decide to walk home although it's nearly two miles; but better than facing further humiliation. On the route home, there's a high fence outside a garage, often illicitly used by children as a climbing frame. It's a bit dangerous, but health and safety are not big concerns. I take off my blouson, hanging it on a nearby post and clamber up the fence, triumphantly reaching the summit. At least one positive result from my otherwise tragic day. I also, daringly, jump from half way down the frame, managing to fall over onto a patch of oil in the garage forecourt. My new corduroy trousers are soiled and slightly torn, probably irreparably? I go over to retrieve my blouson, but whilst trying to unhook it from the post, it accidentally falls behind the adjacent wall. 'Oh dear, what a pity.' I continue my trudge home.

* * *

'Why can't I have long trousers, Mum?' I plead. 'Everyone else has.'
'No they don't' retorts Mother. 'I saw Frank Watson yesterday. He was wearing short trousers.'
'But he's younger than me' I persist. 'Simon Wilkinson changed to long trousers over a month ago.'
This stops Mother in her tracks. The Wilkinson family are highly regarded, the father being an accountant and mother noted for her smart and fashionable dress sense. They live in a slightly up-market house; private, terraced, and quite large. Front room, lace curtains. Mother says nothing for a few days whilst she investigates the evidence.

'We'll go to the Co-op on Saturday and buy you some long trousers. But they have to be smart and you better not dirty or spoil them.'

* * *

Trouser leg width is a critical issue for a fourteen year old boy. My 'keks' are relatively baggy and I want them narrowed to at least '15s' or, even better, '14s'; but I know Mother won't allow it. In her mind, narrow trousers are associated with 'Teddy Boys' as she doesn't distinguish between the 'drain pipe' trousers worn by the latest teenage rebels and the wider '15s'. Knowing there's no point in asking, I go along to the Co-op tailoring department to have them narrowed in secret. My Father's President of *Colne and District Co-operative Society*, so the Department Manager assumes my request is with parental permission. His mistake. I finance the alterations with money from my Sunday paperound.

In the evening we're sitting in the front room watching television. Father and Brother are out at the British Legion where Len's in a local 'Golden Cue' snooker match'; the semi-final, so Mother and I are alone. I sit in an armchair, legs stretched out, heels resting on a low stool, my newly narrowed trousers clearly outlined by the glow from the coal fire.

'Mum, please let me have my trousers narrowed. Only to 15s', I craftily beg. Mother looks over at my well-presented trouser leg.

'No, they're just right as they are' she naively answers. I don't enlighten her.

A later television news report focuses on the visit to Britain by Russian President, Nikita Khrushchev. As a dedicated communist, Mother's fully supportive of his Regime and admires Khrushchev, as she did the previous President, Joseph Stalin. Khrushchev is filmed entering a Foreign Ministry building in London for a meeting with government officials. The TV reporter comments: 'President Khrushchev looks much smarter than when he arrived in the UK. He's wearing a modern suit with a wide lapelled jacket and narrower, well pressed trousers.'

Game, set and match!

* * *

'Never felt more like singin' the blues, 'cos I never thought that I'd ever lose your love, dear. Why'd ye treat me this way?'

I sing the latest pop song whilst admiring myself in the full length wardrobe mirror. A new outfit, light grey, almost white, raglan sleeve jacket with maroon trimmings, the envy of all my friends. I'd wanted a pair of blue denim jeans, but Mother wouldn't have that; too Americanized. But the black, tailored jeans I'm wearing are almost as fashionable. Socks are luminous yellow, also the latest fashion. Len has spent half an hour styling my blond hair, combing out some curls and building a pointed quiff of brylcreemed perfection. I continue singing and looking in the mirror, this time playing a pretend air guitar.

Dedicated Follower of Fashion

'Never felt more like cryin' all night, cos everything's wrong an' nothin' ain't right without you. You've got me singin' the blues.'
'Roy, are you ready?' Mother shouts from the bottom of the stairs. 'We're going to miss the bus if you don't hurry up.'
This brings me back to earth, realising I'm not to appear on stage performing to adoring fans after all. No, I'm going to Nelson on the bus with my Mother to buy a new school uniform. Putting on my dark blue, crepe soled shoes, I bound down the stairs. Walking hurriedly up Skipton Road towards the bus stop, I keep several yards behind, not wanting to be seen with Mother. The bus has just arrived so we dash to get on board. At the same time two teenage girls jump on looking at me and turning to each other laughing and giggling. 'It's because I'm with my Mother' I think to myself, my face reddening.

But, no!
'It's Tommy Steele' they gasp.

* * *

I gaze longingly at the window display in the tailoring department of Colne Co-operative Society. Normally the Co-op's not regarded as a leader of fashion, but a new manager's trying to change that image. In the display is a male mannequin dressed in the latest Italian style suit. Three cloth covered buttons, fastening high up on the 'shorty' jacket, narrow lapels, dark blue and black striped, slightly shiny material. Breast pocket reveals three points of a fake handkerchief; bright pink. Trousers are shaped and narrow, slightly flared, without turnups. A black boot-lace tie and starched white shirt with button-down collar completes the outfit. I'm bewitched.

A few days later I arrive at the department store again, but this time with my Mother, and to the shoe department as new shoes are needed. Luckily, the tailoring department manager's also in charge of shoe sales and has introduced the latest fashions in footwear. As we enter the shop my eyes light up at the sight of a pair of 'winkle pickers'. These Italian style shoes are all the rage with long tapered leather uppers coming to a point quite distant from slightly raised 'Cuban' heels. To crown it all the shoes have shiny brass buckles on the side. The chances of Mother buying me this particular pair of shoes seem remote, but the sales assistant comes to my rescue.

'Mrs Kershaw, these are quality shoes made from real leather, including the soles. None of these new plasticy materials; they'll last for years. Mrs Wilkinson has just bought a pair for her son, Simon.' I doubt that this is true, Simon Wilkinson not being remotely fashion conscious, but who am I to argue? Mother picks up the shoes, examining them closely.

'They don't look comfortable to me. They're very flashy, too' she remarks. 'Try them on, Roy.'

Squeezing the shoes on, I walk across the carpeted floor. They're uncomfortable and my toes feel like they've been wedged into a sardine tin, though I smile, pretending to walk without pain or discomfort.

'They're perfect' I fib. 'Please let me have them, Mum.'

'OK, this time, but don't let me see you swanking in them. You can only wear them for best.'

Mother puts on her sternest expression but I discern not a little pride in a son that's up with the latest teenage fashions. After all, the shoes have been bought from the Co-op, so they can't be bad.

I continue to fantasize about the Italian suit. Though successful with the shoes, my luck's unlikely to continue, so another strategy is needed as I must have the suit in time for the end of term dance at school. I've my eye on a blonde. She's a bit common, and sure to be impressed with my 'Mod' outfit. 'Mods' out-perform 'Rockers' in the fashion stakes, don't they?

How to buy the suit is my problem? I've no money in the bank, or anywhere else for that matter. Although a Sunday paperound is quite well paid, and a one evening a week job collecting Weavers Union dues brings in a small commission, saving for the suit would take too long. I'd lose my chance with the much sought after blonde. Returning to the tailoring department, I browse around the readymade suits on the display racks. Even the cheapest are around £10, far too expensive.

'Can I help you, sir?' enquires the sales assistant.

'How much is the Italian suit in the window?' I ask.

'Only £15, it's in the sale at present.' I listen to the usual salesman's patter. Only £15. That's too much for me.

Dedicated Follower of Fashion

'I'll speak to the Manager and see what we can do' the assistant says helpfully, keeping an eye on his commission.

He goes over to speak to his boss who looks in my direction, clearly recognising me as the Co-op President's son. I return his glance with a friendly but pleading smile. All's fair in my quest for the Italian suit as the sales assistant returns.

'The Manager says that one way to pay for the suit is by joining the Co-op Credit Club. You can pay for it over 15 weeks at £1 per week.' I calculate that if I spend less on beer and records and miss the next three Burnley matches, it should be doable. 'I'll take it.' The suit's hung on a plastic hanger, carefully folded into a large bag with Colne Co-operative Tailoring Department emblazoned on the side. The sales assistant slips the bootlace tie into the bag as a bonus as I sign the credit club card and cram it into my pocket. Now all I have to do is venture home. Hiding the dodgy suit in my bedroom wardrobe, I deliberate when the best time might be to let the cat, or rather the suit, out of the bag. Mother's not going to be happy as she abhors the 'buy now, pay later' syndrome. Over the next few days I constantly come up with reasons for not disclosing my purchase. Doing the washing up without being asked; practicing the piano every evening; cleaning my shoes, all ploys to ingratiate myself, though still not plucking up the necessary courage.

In the event, the decision's taken out of my hands. Returning from a shopping trip to the Co-op, Mother bursts into the living room fuming, heading in my direction, arms raised, feet swinging like a prize fighter. I've never seen her so angry. The thought 'Mother's not going to be happy' turns out to be the understatement of the year. I quickly move out of harm's way.

'Mr Broughton says you've bought a new suit from his department' shouts Mother. 'Where did you get the money from for that?' she cries.

'I joined the Co-op Credit Club' comes my reply from behind the couch. Mother calms down a little at this and, unusually, Len comes to my defence.

'Leave him alone, Mum. He's shown initiative and it's a really smart suit. If he comes up short with the money, I'll help him out.' Mother recognises a *fait accompli* when she sees one.

* * *

A few weeks later it's the end of term dance at Colne Grammar School where I'm now in the 6th form. Arriving early, I look round for Barbara, the blonde I fancy and in whom I've invested so much, both financially and emotionally. She's nowhere to be seen. A couple of other girls come up to me, admiring my Italian suit and shoes, but I'm not interested.

'Have you seen Barbara' I ask one of her friends. 'Is she coming to the dance?'

'Yes, she is, but I think she's coming with Chuddy.' replies Helen with an unsympathetic smirk. I don't believe her.

An hour later there's a kafuffle at the main entrance to the school. Going outside, I find the Headmaster remonstrating with another student who sits astride a powerful motorbike, revving the engine for all it's worth. He's dressed in shiny black leathers with a black visored helmet.

'Chudwick, turn the engine off on that infernal machine. You know you're not allowed to come to school on a motorbike. And you can't come into the dance dressed like that, either' shouts the headmaster.

With all the noise of the Triumph bike it's unlikely the message has got through. I don't know whether it has or not, since all I care about is the sight of Chuddy, resplendent on a powerful motorbike with a blonde pillion passenger, also in leathers.

So much for my Italian suit.

CHAPTER 4

Music, Music, Music

Father takes charge of Sunday mornings. Breakfast in bed for Mother as she enjoys a well-earned lie-in. I'd also like to stay in bed, under warm, snug layers of blankets and flock eiderdown, but am not allowed to.

'Get up, Roy. You'll become demoralised' shouts Mother.

It's unfair, but my protests go unheeded so I get up. Father has lit the fire using the gas poker, connected to the gas supply by a long rubber pipe stretching from kitchen to living room. Not as easy as it sounds as it's not unusual for pipe and poker to become separated, gas seeping into the room and, on occasions, the end of the pipe catching fire. Top quality anthracite coal has warmed the room, providing a welcoming glow. Mouth-watering smells of fried bacon and eggs, freshly brewed coffee (Co-op 'Frescof' grain coffee) drift from the kitchen. A fresh farmhouse loaf with Co-op 'Avondale' butter; thick, creamy Channel Island milk. Father's cooked breakfast and is beginning to prepare Sunday lunch; roast pork, bread and butter pudding.

Paul Robeson's deep, rich tones reverberate from the recently purchased Co-op brand 'Defiant' Radiogram. A VHF radio and record player, enclosed in a shiny, veneered wood cabinet, brings sound quality second to none. Two-Way Family Favourites, on the BBC Light Programme, is broadcasting record requests from our armed forces in Germany. Captivating music awakens deep emotions making hairs stand up on the nape of my neck: *'Just a'wearyin for you, all the time a'feeling blue'* sings Robeson, words folding into the music. The next request's for Kathleen Ferrier singing *'Blow the Wind Southerly'*. Kathleen's *our* family's favourite, being an unspoilt Lancashire Lass from nearby Blackburn. *'Ebb Tide'*, a comedy record by Jerry Colona, is next followed by the soaring strings of *'Cavalier Rusticana'*, holding me spellbound.

Light Programme entertainment doesn't stop there. *'The Billy Cotton Band Show'* follows. *'Wakey, Wakey'* comes the cry from the radio, followed by jolly music and corny, though mirthful jokes. *'Hancock's Half Hour'* is full of deadpan humour, playing on Tony Hancock's lofty ambitions and pomposity, pricked by his own painful shortcomings. The most hilarious programme is *'Educating Archie'*. A comedy show, on radio, based on the antics of a wooden ventriloquist's dummy, seems unlikely; but it works. Father and I roll with laughter.

* * *

'We're getting a piano' Mother announces in a firm voice. 'My dad always said he would, but never did. I'm determined that doesn't happen with me.'

Sure enough, a few days later a second-hand, good quality piano arrives at the house. There's a big problem getting the instrument into our small living room and a door has to be taken off its hinges, causing much cursing and swearing by the workmen; words I've never heard before. Mother berates them. They continue working in silence. The piano can't be put against the window wall of the living room. Another wall has an enclave, not wide enough for the piano and which, anyway, accommodates Mother's much loved Welsh Dresser. A third wall incorporates a coal fire, as well as a door leading into the kitchen, so the only possible place left is the 'party wall' with our neighbours. There's already friction between our families because of noise from two active boys, our neighbours being older and childless. But Mother won't listen to any criticism, so soon there's no communication at all with next door.

Len's first to take piano lessons, from a well-known teacher in Colne, Mrs Gott. He's musical, but when it comes to practicing, it's a different matter with any excuse being used to avoid piano practice. Football training and fitness runs have priority. A few minutes at the piano and practice stops to examine a developing facial spot in the mirror; and he invariably has to go to the toilet in mid-practice. Nevertheless, Len continues with lessons, though not much progress is made.

'Went to the pictures last night to see *'The Great Caruso'*. I'm sure our Len was there, on the balcony' Mother informs Father. 'His piano

Music, Music, Music

lesson was at seven o'clock, so I don't know how he got to the cinema so quickly. That teacher doesn't give enough time to him; no wonder he's not doing very well.' It doesn't occur to Mother that her adored son might not even have been to the lesson.

Another teacher's found in Earby, a bus ride from Colne. Rennie Pawson's well known in the area as an accomplished pianist, almost concert level. However, though lessons last a few more months, sporting activities continue to interfere with piano practice, so eventually they are discontinued. Mother doesn't believe in flogging a dead horse.

I begin lessons with Mr Pawson and, taking to the piano more than Len, and not being distracted by too many sporting activities, good progress is made. My teacher inspires me by playing Beethoven's *Pathetique Sonata*. Mother buys an LP of Chopin Nocturnes, played regularly on our radiogram. However, practice remains a problem even for me. Piano lessons are on Monday evenings and I leave the house at six, catching a bus at the bottom of the street, returning home about eight. Mother and Father are usually watching *'The World at War'* on a black and white television and don't pay much attention to my return, being engrossed with events so close to their own wartime experiences. The problem is that I put off practicing most of the week, trying to catch up on arriving home from school Monday afternoon. Mr Pawson has entered me for Skipton Music Festival and the piece I have to play is quite difficult. On this particular Monday, I haven't practised at all through the week, with no progress on the Festival piece. Unable to face my teacher, I decide to miss the lesson. Leaving the house as usual, I catch the bus to Earby, but then walk round the small town before returning home at the normal time.

'How's the Festival piece coming along? asks Mother. 'Haven't heard you play it much lately.'

'Yes, it's a bit difficult, but I'm getting better' is my less than truthful reply.

Next Monday follows the same pattern as I get deeper and deeper into the mire though the following week I make a recovery, practicing every day, so that by the third Monday I feel confident enough to return to my lesson. 'How's my two weeks absence to be explained?' I ponder. A devious brain, well-honed in thinking up schemes to avoid conflict with Mother, soon comes up with a solution. An Elastoplast wrapped round an index finger will do the trick.

However, the following Monday brings a shock as Len decides to accompany me to renew his acquaintance with Mr Pawson. We sit in the comfortable front room, chatting amiably about Len's progress as a sportsman and what he's been doing since lessons stopped. Then the conversation turns to me.

'It's a pity Roy's had a problem with his finger and not able to come to lessons' Mr Pawson pointedly comments to Len. I freeze in my position on the piano stool. Len of course knows I haven't had a problem with my finger and, until now, has been curious about the Elastoplast that's suddenly made an appearance.

'Yes it is. You trapped it in the door, didn't you, Roy?' Len responds. I breathe a sigh of relief.

It's nearing the date of my appearance at Skipton Music Festival. I'm doing well at the selected piece, but already dreading what would be my first public performance.

'You're on at three in the afternoon a week on Wednesday' warns Mr Pawson. 'You'll have to get time off school.'

I can see this being a problem since Colne has its own Music Festival, permission usually being given for time off to attend this, being in Lancashire. But Skipton's in Yorkshire and inter-county hostility is likely to play a part in the decision. Knocking on the headmaster's door, I stand nervously in the corridor. My relationship with Mr Phillips is not good. He's a frustrated would-be public school headmaster who's had to settle for a smallish grammar school. He hasn't forgiven me for being the only pupil to fail his speech training classes as I mulishly refused to lose a strong Lancashire accent. My family's working-class credentials add to a mutual antipathy.

'Yes, Kershaw. What do you want?' the Headmaster asks brusquely through the half open door.

'I need time off school next Wednesday to perform at Skipton Music Festival. It's on the piano.'

Mr Phillips looks at me with cold, stony eyes. 'No!' comes the abrupt, contemptuous reply, the door closing with a sharp thump. Feelings of resentment stir, but these are ameliorated by relief that I won't have to perform in public.

So ends my budding (in Mother's eyes) career as a concert pianist.

Music, Music, Music

* * *

'I dreamed I saw Joe Hill last night,
alive as you and me.
Says I 'But Joe, you're ten years dead.'
'I never died' said he,
'I never died' said he.

'The Copper Bosses killed you Joe,
they shot you Joe' says I.
'Takes more than guns to kill a man.'
Says Joe 'I didn't die.'
Says Joe 'I didn't die.'

Mother softly sings this well-loved song as she dusts and polishes her precious ornaments. The song encapsulates her strong union ideology, and is particularly loved since it's sung on an oft' played record by Paul Robeson, the black American Communist. Paul Robeson had performed the song at a Welsh Miner's Union gathering some years before, an event that had a lasting impact on our family, combining union solidarity, socialist principles and anti-racism within a rich, soulful bass voice. Mother had also been to hear him at St. George's Hall in Bradford, an event she often talks about.

'Paul Robeson has an incredible voice, full of depth and pathos. He sang *'Song of Peace'*; really Beethoven's *'Ode to Joy'*, but with the words changed.' Mother takes a breath, voice trembling with emotion. 'He also spoke strongly of how he'd learned his militancy and politics from our own Labour Movement. Can't remember the full words, but it was something like 'the fight of Negros in America is like the fight of oppressed workers everywhere. It's the same struggle.'

Another much-loved Paul Robeson recording is *'Ma Curly Headed Baby'*, but it's not much loved by me. My blond curly hair's an embarrassment and I dread the record being played, particularly when aunts are visiting. Fortunately the record's now owned not by Mother, but one of her sisters, Aunty Ida. We don't see much of Ida, partly because she lives in Blackburn, some distance away from Colne, but mainly because Ida has been figuratively sent even further away – to Coventry. Marrying the manager of a Boots branch, one of the Co-op's competitors, has put her beyond the pale in Mother's eyes, so we seldom visit Ida and her family, and she seldom visits us. As a result there are few opportunities to play the record, even though it remains a family favourite. Some years later I'm to be reacquainted with *'Ma Curly Headed Baby'*, though not in a good way.

'Roy, your Aunty Ida phoned. She's giving you her radiogram for a wedding present' Mother informs me, with some reluctance. 'You'd better go over there and pick it up.'

I ask to borrow Len's car, a Rover 60 with a big boot. In fact I'm forced to beg, having pranged the vehicle on two previous occasions, but as there's no alternative means to collect the gift, a promise 'to be more careful' persuades Len, against his better judgement, to give me the keys. The following day I drive round to pick up Janet, my fiancé, and we set off for Blackburn. Janet doesn't have much confidence in my driving, but this is made up for by my own over-confidence as prior accidents haven't raised doubts in my own mind about my driving skills. Aunty Ida's terraced house isn't as opulent as I'd expected of a Boots Branch Manager, so the idea Ida's sold out to the capitalist private sector doesn't ring true. We park the Rover at the roadside, climb a short flight of steps and knock on a newly painted front door. It's opened by an effusive Ida.

'Wonderful to see you, Roy. And this must be your fiancé, Janet?' She spills out the words with genuine delight. 'So glad you could make it, and congratulations on your engagement.'

We sit down for a cup of tea whilst Ida continues to make us feel welcome and cherished. 'Why has politics been allowed to split our family and kept us away from this loving Aunt?' I wonder.

The radiogram's large and we struggle to carry it down the narrow steps, though eventually manage, loading it into the open boot of the Rover.

'Wait there, Roy' orders Ida, who dashes back into the house, returning with an old 78" vinyl record in a tatty brown paper cover. 'This is a record of Paul Robeson singing Ma Curly Headed Baby' Ida enthusiastically informs us. 'We've had it for years. It's become a family heirloom so I think you should have it since you're the one with curls in the family.'

I manage to hide my disappointment with this unexpected gift.

Music, Music, Music

Janet puts it on the front passenger seat of the car as we continue thanking Ida for the radiogram and her kind words. I open the car door for Janet to get in, and walk round to the driver's side. But as I do, there's a sharp cracking sound as Janet sits on the 'family heirloom'. Ida doesn't appear to have heard it and we manage to maintain our frozen smiles, waving energetically as I pull away from the kerb. Emotions are mixed. A long-term embarrassment's been removed; but so has an irreplaceable memento of a unique bass voice.

* * *

It's Wednesday evening and I go to bed early, not because I'm tired, but so I can listen to Juke Box Hits on Radio Luxembourg. My radio's old, a vintage Bush valve radio in an Art-Deco cabinet. It looks good on the bedside table, though that's about all, taking an age to warm up as I try tuning to 208 metres medium wave. BBC's Light Programme and Third Programme come through loud and clear, though no such luck with Radio Luxembourg. Reception's poor, much fading and crackling, but since there's little pop music on the BBC, I persevere with the commercial station. By propping up a pillow next to the bedside table I can lie with my ear pressed to the side of the radio cabinet. Not ideal, but it's the best I can do.

'Hello, Pop Pickers.' The enthusiastic, inimitable voice of Alan Freeman transmits over the air waves. 'Here are your top twenty records brought to you by Horace Batchelor and his famous Infra-Draw Method. Using this system you're guaranteed to win big money on the Pools.'

At 20 it's Johnnie Ray with *'Just Walkin' in the Rain'*. Reception fades, but I don't mind, not being a big fan of Johnnie Ray with his feigned crying. Other records follow: Bill Haley and His Comets with *'See you later, Alligator'*; Little Richard's *'Long, Tall Sally'*; Pat Boone's *'Love Letters in the Sand'*; Paul Anka singing his own composition, *'Diana'*.

'Bye Bye Love. Bye Bye Happiness. Hello Loneliness, I wish that I could die-ie.' The Everley Brothers are at number ten. I'd watched them the evening before on the Perry Como show, the first TV pop show to come from America. My ear remains glued to the radio as I listen for the number one hit which I'm expecting to be Elvis Presley

with *'All Shook Up'*; and it is. Reception doesn't fade and there's no crackling. Heaven!

The previous weekend, we'd been to see Elvis in his first film *'Love Me Tender'*.

'Well there's a hole in the roof where the rain pours in
A hole in the floor, where it drops right out again.'

A black and white film doesn't detract from an exhilarating vision of Elvis, in jeans and open-necked shirt, singing about a poor southern white working-class farm family. Hips gyrate, legs shake, shiny jet black hair swirls as he plays his acoustic guitar in an old, broken down shack. Turning off the radio, I sing myself to sleep under the bed covers.

'Well, blessa ma soul, what's wrong with me. Am shaking like a man on a fuzzy tree. Friends say I'm acting wild as a bug. I'm in love; I'm all shook up.' I dream of being on stage, playing a guitar and singing to screaming fans.

* * *

Pop songs continue to dominate my musical life, *New Musical Express* providing news and gossip as well as the latest charts. In addition, a school friend, Peter, and I design our own Pop Chart. Peter's a genius at creating competitions and interesting indoor games. A *Subuteo League* in which we have our own teams of small plastic football figures (my team's Blackpool, being a fan of Stanley Matthews). These are flicked around a table size cloth football pitch chasing a tiny plastic ball. *Howzat* is another game, this time cricket, where small metal, octagonal dice-like pieces are rolled to determine how many runs each of us score, and how we are dismissed; 'Howzat!'

The best wheeze though is our home-made Pop Chart, which consists of a half-quarto size piece of card with twenty small slits into which are inserted the top ten pop songs, written on slivers of card. On the reverse of the slivers are recorded the number of times we hear a particular tune on the radio during the week. The number of 'hearings' of a recording determines its position in the chart. On Fridays we compare charts, hoping our preferred singers are at the top. Adam Faith and

Music, Music, Music

Buddy Holly are my favourites, Pat Boone and Jimmie Rogers are Peter's. Mysteriously the charts differ, 'Number Ones' usually corresponding with our own particular pop idols.

* * *

An advert in the NME catches my eye.

> **Northern Floating Jazz Festival**
> Heysham to Isle of Man Ferry, Saturday 20th June
> Acker Bilk / Kenny Ball / Chris Barber plus other Jazz Greats

'Not to be missed' I tell myself and rush off to inform my friends at Rabanos Coffee Bar. Traditional Jazz is at peak popularity and we regularly visit Thornton Manor Jazz Club on Sunday nights. I long to go to the Beaulieu Jazz Festival, but it's too expensive, so the Northern Floating Jazz Festival seems a suitable, cheaper alternative. As things work out only four of us, David, Malcolm, Graham and me make it to Heysham Head. As we board, I'm apprehensive since on two previous trips to the Isle of Man, seasickness had overwhelmed me; but today's calm and sunny so hopefully this won't be a problem. As soon as we board the steamer there's a feeling we don't belong. We're dressed in what might be described as 'Mod' suits – narrowish trousers, short three buttoned jackets, narrow lapels; all very smart. Other passengers, mostly beatniks, wear anything they like. Scruffy, tie-dyed T-shirts printed with slogans: 'Make Love Not War'; 'Flower Power', along with CND logo designs and other anti-establishment messages. Tight blue jeans, full of holes; track suit bottoms; worn-out moccasins. Bohemian behaviour matches their Bohemian dress code. Smoking what we believe to be 'reefers' (drugs haven't yet reached our home town); lugubrious dancing to their own beat; drinking beer, cider, wine on deck. Lifestyles that are unfamiliar but offer an attractive image of complete freedom. We move below deck to listen to the bands. Acker Bilk, bearded, short stature playing his 'liquorice stick' with gusto. The lively sound of joyful jazz trumpet from Kenny Ball and more sophisticated, soulful tones of Chris Barber's trombone.

It all adds up to more than two hours of Trad Magic.

Disembarking at the ferry port in Douglas, I find myself walking alongside Acker Bilk; shiny striped waistcoat and angled bowler hat. He's with his partner, who's about a foot taller than him, wearing a loose fitting, ethnic-patterned dress; buxom and exotic. 'Funny looking fuckin' boat' he says to me in a broad West Country accent. I don't understand what he means, but laugh anyway. Really with the in-crowd now!

* * *

'Two-Way Family Favourites' had been an introduction to classical music, but Mother is my inspiration. She encourages me to watch and listen to operas and other music programmes on television. Eric Robinson's *'Music for You'* brings a wide variety of high'ish brow entertainment: *'Chorus of the Hebrew Slaves'* from Verdi's Nabucco; *'The Nuns' Chorus'* from Casanova by Strauss; Ian Wallace sings *'The Hippopotamus Song'* (Mud, Mud, Glorious Mud) and *The Flea Song* by Mussorgsky. BBC TV excels with live Opera. We listen to *'Pagliacci'* by Ruggero Leoncavallo, tears trickle down both our faces as Pagliaccio sings *'On with the motley, the paint and the powder'*, donning clown's costume, applying clown's make-up, whilst morosely contemplating his wife's infidelity.

Grieg's *'Peer Gynt Suite'* is full of exciting, provocative music: dark, rhythmic *'In the Hall of the Mountain King'*; bright, optimistic *'Morning'*; mournful, moving *'Solveig's Song'*. Mother buys the piano score in the hope I'll be able to play it. Remarkably, I can; the music's an 'easy-play' version. *'Porgy and Bess'* is riveting. From Bess' delicate lullaby *'Summertime'*; through Porgy's happy-go-lucky *'I got plenty o'nuttin'*; romantic love songs *'Bess, You is My Woman Now'* and *'I Loves You, Porgy'*; lively, blasphemous *'It Ain't Necessarily So'*; to the determined, husky *'Oh, Lawd, I'm on my way'* as Porgy sets off to find his Bess. The Gershwin opera's an emotional roller coaster ride. Mother reminds me that Paul Robeson had refused the role of Porgy because it 'perpetuated stereotypes of black Americans of a bygone era'.

I buy my first classical record, an e.p. of the Grieg Piano Concerto, giving it to Mother as a birthday present. A few days later I come home to find her lying on the couch listening to the record, deeply moved; in tears.

Mr Land arranges a school trip to Manchester Free Trade Hall to hear the Concerto performed by the Hallé Orchestra. I act blasé, not wanting to betray a liking for classical music in front of pop-loving friends. Only three of us have signed up for the concert trip, so Mr Land takes us in his own car, a Hillman Minx. Our seats on the balcony overlook the orchestral stage. The Hall's magnificent, ornately decorated; gilded organ-pipes at the back of the stage; plush red velvet seats stretching upwards to 'the Gods'; an atmosphere of self-confidence. The auditorium's full, with an audience of eclectic mix, some men in evening suits, others in woolly jumpers – most with long hair. Bejewelled, matronly ladies accompany the 'suits'; trousered, earnest women the 'jumpers'. Very old, old, middle aged, young, very young; all ages. But mainly old.

Orchestral players swarm onto the stage like black beetles. Men wear dress trousers, black cummerbunds and bow ties; smart black skirts and white blouses for female instrumentalists. The 'strings' settle at the front; violins, violas, cellos. Gentle wind instruments take their places behind; flutes, oboes, clarinets. At the back, pompous brass; trumpets, trombones, tubers, polished instruments glistening in the bright spotlights. Imperious kettle drums overlook the whole orchestra, with percussionists waiting to awaken anyone who dares to fall asleep.

Orchestra and auditorium are silent, then polite applause ripples as the lead violinist strides across the stage. Silence returns until the entrance of a short, thick-set craggy faced conductor, with a deep, serious frown. He steps onto the raised, railed-in platform as clapping increases in volume. Silence again; then enthusiastic applause as the piano soloist appears, a small wiry man with a shock of steely silver hair. An appearance of quiet reserve changes to charismatic charm as he turns to the audience, acknowledging his welcome with a wide, appreciative smile and modest bow.

Without delay, the orchestra bursts into life, as a dramatic timpani roll leads to an even more dramatic piano flourish. Gnarled fingers scurry up and down the keyboard; steely hair rises and falls as powerful chords ring out. Then the orchestra calms down as the wind section introduces glimpses of a sonorous melody. In the second movement the piano brings out the melody in full; sad, melancholy bringing me close to tears. The final movement sweeps away the sombre mood with orchestra and piano vying with each other to play the most joyful, dance-like themes. The Concerto ends on a high for both orchestra and audience with a rapturous ovation following the final notes. Our soloist bows energetically and the conductor lifts his arms, encouraging the whole orchestra to rise in salute. Conductor and soloist leave the stage, but make two more appearances before applause dies down. The audience drifts away, some to the bar, some to chat with other concert goers. We remain seated without talking as I read through the programme to find out more.

The second half of the concert is to be a Symphony; Brahms' Fourth which I've never heard before. The audience settles down and all's quiet except for bouts of coughing punctuating the silence; better now than during the performance. The leader of the orchestra bounces onto the stage again, greeted by exuberant clapping, swiftly followed by the conductor, face still rugged and stern. Without ceremony he lifts his baton.

Romantic, tender violins open with silvery, shimmering sounds joined by bassoons and other woodwind. Cellos and muted brass enter and several themes sing out at the same time, not competing but complementing each other in an harmonious whole; music within music. Flutes and oboes intervene with a jolly, tuneful interlude before the violins return with their insistent drama. Kettle drums are not to be ignored and bring the first movement to a close with a vibrant roll. Then French horns call out the theme, echoed by woodwind and quiet staccato violins. I sit up in my seat straining to see from where this unbelievable sound is coming. Violins and cellos burst out again with a huge melody. Slight delays, as different parts of the orchestra join in, re-emphasising expressive musicality. My body shakes; I begin to sob silently. The words compassion, love and truth filter through my head. The Third Movement brings a happier interlude from violins and woodwind, but sombre moments return with French horns. Exciting violins provide a background as different instruments in the orchestra seem to play to each other. Kettle drums and timpani finish off the Movement as trombones and brass augur in the Finale. Uplifting violins play the melody again, repeated in turn by other instruments. A long passage by flutes seems to sum everything up before dramatic

Music, Music, Music

final statements by the full orchestra brings an unforgettable experience to an electrifying end. For a few seconds there's silence before the whole auditorium erupts into deafening applause and cheers. Shouts of 'Bravo, Bravo' echo round the hall. Everyone stands up, including the grammar school group. The conductor turns to acknowledge the acclaim, but his face remains stern and inscrutable. He exits the platform, returning as applause continues and the whole orchestra stands to delight in the waves of approval. Exit the conductor, but yet again he has to return to his dais. On his fourth re-appearance a slight upturn of the corners of his mouth begins to light up his face, soon turning into a fully-fledged smile.

CHAPTER 5

All You Need is Love

It's a cold, dark winter evening. Although the living room's warmed by a glowing coal fire, the rest of the house is icy, particularly the back lobby which houses the 'lav'. I try to delay an urge for a wee by opening and closing my legs rhythmically, but this doesn't work for long. Venturing through the kitchen and back door into the bare, cement-floored toilet I turn on a single, unshaded light bulb and lift the wooden toilet seat. The Council's done a slap dash job with tiling the walls, some of which have fallen off, whilst others are covered with the dark yellow paint used haphazardly in all council properties. Toilet paper, in the form of small squares of the *Daily Herald*, hangs on a string next to the 'lav'.

I pull down the front of my elasticated shorts to release 'willy' and begin weeing. Both hands are used to control the direction of urine flow because if it gets onto the toilet rim or, even worse, the floor then I'm in trouble. Looking down at 'willy', I wonder why it's so complicated. 'Why don't we just have a hole where the wee comes out?' I ask myself. 'Then there wouldn't be a problem of wee spraying where it shouldn't.' Rehousing my mini private part, I pull up the shorts and go back into the living room. Innocently I ask the same question of Mum and Dad, and Aunty Mary, who's visiting. There's a stunned silence for a few seconds followed by loud guffaws, Aunty Mary laughing with great glee as I stand there in embarrassed silence looking to the floor, face bright red, not understanding the mirth generated. My basic shyness is compounded.

* * *

The wide front room window of our council house overlooks not only Temple Street, but also the adjacent, cobbled Townley and Dickson Streets. Much local activity can be witnessed from this

All You Need is Love

vantage point. Children playing football or cricket on the street; neighbours' families on regular visits; new mothers taking their babies out, pushing large perambulators; householders taking their food and garden waste to the 'pig bins' located at regular intervals down the street. The rag-and-bone man is often there with his horse drawn cart.

At present I'm spending a lot of time looking out of the window in the hope of seeing Nan, a teenage girl visiting a friend of my Mother.

Mrs Lomax works with Mother at the local weaving mill. She lives in a council house across the back gardens of both our properties, but we have to walk up Townley Street to reach the house. It's not done to take a short cut across well-tended gardens.

'We're going up to see Mrs Lomax, Roy' informs Mother. 'Her granddaughter Nan is visiting for a few days. I haven't seen her for years.'

Mother knocks on the back door, which is opened by a rotund Mrs Lomax wearing a flour-flecked pinny, large wooden spoon in hand. She's baking a cake. A tempting country kitchen aroma infuses the air.

'Hello, Martha,' as always, a warm friendly welcome. 'This is my granddaughter, Nan. Bet you don't recognise her.' Mother goes over and gives Nan a hug.

'I certainly don't. She was only a baby the last time I saw her' agrees Mother.

I keep in the background, but watch Nan intently. She's wearing a loose, flowery summer frock, her light auburn fringed hair almost covering sparkling green eyes. A happy smile lights up a healthy, slightly chubby face. Unrecognised feelings stir inside.

'So this is Roy' says Nan. 'What gorgeous curly hair.' She ruffles my curls with a gentle touch. I recoil and blush, eyes averted. 'Oh, look how shy he is' Nan laughs. 'How old is he now?'

'Just turned six' Mother replies.

Mrs Lomax brings over a freshly baked sponge cake with chocolate topping.

'Do you want a piece, Roy?' she asks.

I nod, but don't speak. She cuts off a large slice and puts it on a plate, together with a glass of weak orange cordial. I sit down at the kitchen table to eat the delicious treat. This is one of the reasons I look forward to visiting Mrs Lomax – she's always baking.

Next day, back at home looking out of the window, I catch a glimpse of a flowery dress. It's Nan walking down Townley Street. 'Is she coming to our house?' Eager hopes rise in anticipation, but instead of turning left, she continues walking down the street. Knocking at a door further down, it's opened by a girl about her own age and Nan goes inside. I'm crestfallen.

A few days later I still can't forget Nan. Putting on my coat and shoes I leave the house without telling Mother and walk up to Mrs Lomax's. I knock on the back door with my knuckled hand, unable to reach the knocker. Mrs Lomax pops her head round the partly opened door.

'Oh, it's you Roy. Where's your Mum?' I don't answer.

'I've come to see Nan. Is she in?' Mrs Lomax laughs.

'No, she went back to her house yesterday. She's to go back to school. You'd better go home before your Mum misses you.'

* * *

It's a hot summer afternoon, though a gentle breeze, drifting in from Morecambe Bay, brings a little relief as we walk along the promenade. The tide's out but most of the beach remains hard, wet sand and pebbles. Only one section of the shore has dry, soft sand - near the North Pier, so we head in that direction. Mother buys ice cream, Ninety-Niners, for both of us and we sit on a bench overlooking the sandy beach. The sound of laughter and girly screams comes from the enclave as I walk over and lean on railings at the edge of the prom. Three girls and a boy, a little older than me, but not much older, are throwing a beach ball to each other, running and diving onto the sand. 'Oh, how I'd like to join them' I think to myself, but am much too shy to ask.

However, as I turn to go back and sit with Mother, one of the girls runs up the steps and shouts to me. She's wearing blue and white striped swimming shorts and a loose, sleeveless bright yellow blouse. Strands of short, dark, dishevelled hair stick to her sweat glistened face. Long legs are suntanned, a picture of youthful energy.

'Why don't you come and play with us?' she shouts. I turn away and begin walking towards Mother but the girl persists. 'Don't be a softy' she admonishes me. Quickly running across, she grabs my arm and pulls me towards the steps.

All You Need is Love

'Yes, go and play, Roy. We're not in any hurry' encourages Mother. No longer able to resist, I succumb and join their games on the beach. There don't seem to be any rules to the game. The beach ball's thrown towards the incoming tide and we all dash, trying to be first to catch it. There's much tripping, pulling of shirts and falling in the sand. I'm the fastest, but another boy pulls me back by my shorts. As he runs towards the ball, I manage to grab his ankle, bringing him to ground. My friendly girl in the yellow blouse nips in and triumphantly picks up the beach ball. All the games are played with boisterous good humour, and much laughing and giggling. It's one of the few times I've enjoyed uninhibited fun. Mother shouts.

'Roy, you'll have to come back now. We're going to the pictures so need to get a bite to eat first.' I'm in a buoyant, even ecstatic mood as I wave goodbye to my new found friends.

'It's Great to be Young' starring John Mills advertises the poster outside the cinema. Mother's attracted to the film by one of her favourite actors, but I'm not so keen, preferring cowboy or space adventure films. The cinema's nearly empty so we can sit almost anywhere. I head for the front seats though Mother insists we sit further back; but at least I'm allowed a packet of *'Butterkist'*.

The film turns out to be eminently enjoyable. The story concerns a school band threatened with closure because the music teacher, played by John Mills, is too involved in popular music for the new head teacher's taste. Various misdemeanours lead to his dismissal, which the student band members decide to fight. An entertaining storyline and I've great empathy with the students since I'm learning to play the piano and keen on all types of music. There's also another storyline; a romantic one. A girl and boy in the band are attracted to each other and fall in love, eventually. I laugh out loud at the end of the film when they trip up – into each other's arms. Mother glances at me with a quizzical expression. 'Is he growing up?' the look seems to say. The film's theme tune, *'You are My First Love'* sung by Ruby Murray, clutches at heart strings.

The next day I persuade Mother to return to the sandy beach in the hope of seeing my yellow-bloused new friend. But there's nobody there.

* * *

My love life's a struggle!

I'm a quite good looking boy and blond curly hair seems to attract younger girls in the school. But these girls don't attract me, either because they're too young and giggly or downright 'Plain Janes', so I search elsewhere. My first target's June Parker who lives on Dickson Street, only a hundred yards from my own house. I hear June's having a birthday party, but I'm not invited. Playing in the street outside her house, kicking a football against the wall, doesn't result in my being asked in. I buy a Valentine's card, put it in an envelope and seal it with S.W.A.L.K. Having addressed the envelope, I post it in the red GPO pillar box. Too late! I fail to put a stamp on it.

Not giving up, however, I wait at the bottom of the cobbled back street, watching out for June alighting from the school bus. She walks up the street with a friend as I cycle up to them.

'Will you go out with me? I manage to blurt out. This results in June's friend bursting into laughter, but my hoped for date takes it more seriously.

'Can't; already going out with Heyworth' she replies.

I turn round on my bike and disconsolately ride away. Heyworth's two forms above me at school, and also centre forward in the football team. I can't compete with that.

* * *

It's the end of term exams. I'm in the 4th form, sitting at my desk awaiting the exam paper. We share the classroom with pupils from the 5th Form who come in and join us. A tall, very slim blonde girl sits at a desk just in front of me. Her navy blue school uniform's a little large, draped over an awkward, angular frame. A pale, pretty face, without any makeup, reveals a gentle, shy smile. I'm captivated. A few days later another 5th form girl sidles up to me as I walk along the corridor to my next lesson.

'Ann Peters likes you' she whispers. 'Will you go out with her?' I'm non-committal at this unexpected approach, not even realising Ann Peters has noticed me. 'She'll meet you outside the Palace at six o'clock on Saturday.' I mumble something incoherent as the girl drifts away. I'm nonplussed.

All You Need is Love

Father, Mother and I relax, watching the black and white television in the corner of the living room. Saturday night programmes are enjoyable; scary *Quatermass and the Pit*; friendly *Dixon of Dock Green*; Mike and Bernie Winters *Variety Show* with Alma Cogan providing the vocals. There's a knock at the front door and I go to answer it.

'I was waiting for you at the cinema. Where were you?' Ann asks sweetly but accusingly.

She looks very pretty with makeup and a pink ribbon in her short blond hair. There's a tremor in her voice as she tries to fight back tears. I'm dumfounded and begin trying to explain that I hadn't realised it was a proper date. But before I can tell her the full story, Mother comes to the door.

'Our Roy doesn't go out with girls at his age' Mother unkindly asserts, not giving her a chance to speak.

Ann blushes; her eyes fill with tears as she turns and hurries down the steps. On Monday there's no sign of Ann, but a message filters through that she's too embarrassed to come to school. So ends what could have been a beautiful relationship.

* * *

'Let's go down The Imp on Saturday' Malcolm whispers during an RI lesson. 'Julie says it's fabulous.'

Malcolm's one of my best mates. As well as being fellow pupils at the grammar school, we play football together for the school team, as well as in the local under 17s league with 'The Saints' football club. Julie's his older sister, a striking redhead with wonderful *joie de vivre*.

We arrive at the Imperial Ballroom at about eight o'clock on Saturday evening. To have enough money for the entrance fee we've had to forego a drink at the local pub. In our best Italian suits, boot lace ties and white, starched collar shirts, we look out of place amongst other more casually dressed teenagers. I feel out of my depth and nervous.

The word 'fabulous' doesn't do justice to the scene before us. A huge, polished dance floor is full of couples, twisting to Chubby Checker's hit record, *The Twist*. Boys in rolled up shirt sleeves vigorously pull, push and swing their partners round in time to the exciting beat of

Chuck Berry's *Let It Rock*. A glittering ball of light rotates slowly in the ceiling, showering dancers with a Milky Way of shimmering speckles. There are more girls than boys, many of them dancing in small circles round their handbags. Back-combed, bee-hive hairdos predominate and faces with too much make-up are full of joy, though heavy mascara is beginning to run down otherwise pretty features. Round the dance floor are large, fur-lined couches. Couples are snogging, wrestling energetically, arms and hands moving in all directions. They don't appear to be sticking with just one partner – it's a case of come one, come all. At one end of the auditorium's a bar, separated from the dance floor by a fabricated framework of Hawaiian style plastic flowers and creepers, the entrance guarded by two muscled 'bouncers'. Being well under eighteen, we don't attempt to go in.

A group of teddy boys crowd round the bar, some of them sitting on ultra-high bar stools. They're all dressed exactly the same, and behave exactly the same. Long, draped brown jackets with pocket flaps and velvet trim collars; drainpipe trousers, short enough to show off luminous green socks; Slim Jim ties and crepe-soled shoes finish off the 'uniform'. Greased-up, Brylcreemed hairstyles have Elvis Presley quiffs, combed to form a 'duck's arse' at the back. We prefer our Italian suits.

We're eager to join the dancers, but can't rock and roll or jive. The only dances learnt at grammar school are the Valeta and Gay Gordons. I don't expect these dances to make an appearance any time soon. Then Julie rushes up to us, grabbing Malcolm by the arm.

'Come on, Malcolm, give it a go. It's easy.'

She pulls him onto the dance floor and starts dragging him round to the beat. Remarkably, Malcolm picks it up quickly and soon looks quite 'cool', though not as animated as other dancers. Julie comes back to us, this time with a friend.

'Vera, this is Malcolm's school mate, Roy. He wants to learn to dance. I'm sure you can teach him.'

Vera is lithe and petite with light brown hair tied into a ponytail. She's pretty, my 'Venus in a ponytail', as I misremember a Bobby Vee song. Feeling overawed I try to move away, mumbling something about going to get a drink, but Vera seizes me with a firm, strong grip and guides me to a space on the dance floor. The thumping beat of *'Long Tall Sally'* pounds through my limbs. I let myself go, helped by

All You Need is Love

a strong lead from an uninhibited Vera. It's a bewitching night at the 'Imp'.

At half past ten my spirits take a downturn. Into the dance hall comes a gang of drunken yobs. Pubs now closed, loutish revellers have arrived for more beer and to pick up any girls they can. A fight starts and soon bouncers appear on the scene. John and I, along with Julie and Vera, leave hurriedly. We don't want to get mixed up with the brawl and, anyway, it's nearly time for the last bus to Colne. My companions are going in the opposite direction, to Brierfield. I don't even wave to Vera since my bus is about to pull out; though running at top speed, I just manage to clasp the platform pole as the bus swings round the corner.

After this successful, thrilling introduction to the world of music, dancing and pretty girls, we continue to frequent the Imp at every opportunity, sometimes with my pals, sometimes with assorted girlfriends. For some reason the Imp becomes even more popular, attracting top Groups of the time: *The Beatles*; *The Rolling Stones*; *The Animals*; *Wee Willy Harris*; *Gene Vincent*. In the Trad Era, all the best jazz combos come: *Chris Barber*; *Acker Bilk*; *Kenny Ball*; *Humphrey Lyttleton*.

* * *

My next hunting ground's the Methodist Youth Club in Colne. A new pupil has joined our class, a tall lanky girl with blazing red hair and fiery personality to match. Beatrice is daughter of the new Methodist Minister and she quickly makes friends with other girls in the class.

'Why don't you come to our youth club down Exchange Street?' Beatrice asks, issuing a general invitation. 'You're only expected to go to Church once a month and even that's not compulsory.'

I'm the only boy to respond to the invitation, being attracted to this engaging newcomer. However, on my first visit to the youth club I'm enticed not by Beatrice, but by a sultry brunette. Linda's not particularly pretty but has large, come-hither brown eyes, with long seductive lashes and I can't help but stare as she climbs onto a high coffee bar stool. Her short, tight skirt rides up as she stretches to reach for the sugar bowl. Putting on a Modern Jazz Quartet LP, I slide over to sit next to her. 'Real 'Cool' – both the music and my approach' I think to myself.

'Do you like the MJQ?' I query.

'I certainly do' comes the reply, voice as seductive as her lashes.

I usually find it hard to look into someone's eyes, but on this occasion manage to overcome my shyness. And what eyes! It's like sinking into a deep pool as warm, lustful feelings stir. Even when other club regulars join us, we can't take our eyes off each other. Hands touch, sending a thrilling current through my testosterone-fueled body. The rest of the evening passes as if in a dream.

A number of dates follow. We go to the cinema on Friday evening to see Cliff Richard in *Expresso Bongo* though don't see much of the film, snogging passionately on the back row. Pat's a football fan so we go to watch Burnley play Swansea at Turf Moor. Burnley win so it's a successful day out, though expensive. We go for a Sunday afternoon walk round Foulridge Reservoir, also called, somewhat pretentiously, Lake Burwain. It's a warm sunny day and the superb scenery of rolling green hills, with Pendle Hill in the background, lulls us towards romantic thoughts as we gravitate to a secluded grassy knoll and lie down. So far our physical attraction has involved mainly kissing and cuddling, not even French kissing. But the balmy afternoon, and a spot hidden by leafy trees, encourages me to take things further. Pat's wearing a white, embroidered blouse buttoned down the front and I reach to unfasten the top button. No resistance, so I continue. My hand moves inside blouse and bra towards her bosom; and my first disappointment. Instead of firm, pointed breasts I'd seen in Playboy Magazines circulating at school, Pat's are fat and floppy; like a double-yolked, sunny-side up fried egg. My ardour ebbs and plans to venture under her skirt are abandoned.

A few weeks later we climb on board a mini-bus outside the Methodist youth club. The Minister's persuaded club members to attend a 'Day of Reflection' at a Retreat Centre in Ilkley, of *'Ilkley Moor b'aht 'at'* fame. Though not interested myself, I'd signed up because Linda was enthusiastic, seeming to be in a period of mildly religious fervour. Activities are supervised by Sisters of the Cross and Passion and the event turns out to be a moving experience. The charismatic Sisters talk about their lives as Nuns with a deeply religious passion, making an emotive impression on all of us. One of the Sisters plays an acoustic guitar, gently singing melodic folk songs, no doubt with hidden messages. We're lulled into an almost hypnotic trance, particularly Linda, who talks intimately to a Sister in a one-to-one session at the end of the 'happening'.

'I think I'll become a Nun' she declares as we reboard the minibus. We sit next to each other, but no longer hold hands. Our eyes meet without any spark; passion's dead. *'Walking back to happiness, woopah oh yeah, yeah, yeah'* sings Helen Shapiro over the minibus radio. We both know this isn't going to happen. A quickly flashed, insincere smile says it all.

* * *

There's also a religious undertone with my next girlfriend. Rita comes from a strongly Catholic family and attends a private Catholic College in Blackburn. She's a pretty, petite brunette with quiet disposition and brown, all-knowing eyes. Her father has a grocery business and the family live in an end terraced private house. Both our fathers are members of the British Legion Club and sometimes play cards together. But that's where cordiality ends. Neither family really approves of our association, though nothing much is said. A relationship between the son of a communist, atheist trade union leader and the daughter of a strongly Catholic, private businessman doesn't augur well.

As it is we enjoy each other's company, dancing down the Imp, drinking with friends round local pubs, joining in at the youth club. Snogging and light petting is not a problem. We don't talk about politics or religion, but the first blip comes when I invite her to the house whilst parents and brother are out. We sit closely together on the sofa watching TV and, putting my arm round her, share a gentle kiss. I squeeze more tightly and begin looking into her eyes. Suddenly Rita starts and pulls away.

'I've to go to Church for eight o'clock' she says. 'It's part of my Re-Confirmation Programme; I have to see my Priest.'

This seems incredulous to me and I feel sure it's just a way of getting out of my clutches. Nevertheless Rita convinces me it's true, so I help to put on her coat and we agree to meet again on the following Friday. However, things are not the same. I begin to be bored.

'Had a super time in Blackpool on Saturday' enthuses David. I'm in the pub with my best mates listening to stories of their exploits over the last couple of weeks. 'Drinking all day, on the dodgems 'til we were banned for too many orchestrated crashes. Largest fish and chips you've ever seen! Girls galore, all ready for a quick necking session. Ted nearly got arrested. He'd brought his unfinished pint out of the pub when we ran to catch the last train back. A Copper stopped him, but instead of apologising, Ted got into an argument. He stood there talking to the policeman with that stupid grin of his. I managed to persuade the Copper to let him go, promising to get him on the train. It was a close shave.'

'The Saturday before was even better' pipes in Tom. 'Went to Batley Variety Club to see Roy Orbison. Really posh club.... much better than the local working men's clubs. It had thick pile carpets with plush velvet chairs and smart tables; plenty of room. We booked an alcove of our own with direct view of the stage, which had amazing gold coloured curtains.' Everybody agrees with the description. 'Then the lights dimmed, everything went quiet, and the curtains slowly opened.'

'Dum-dum-dum-dumdy-doo-wah
Oh-yay-yay-yay-yeah
Oh-oh-oh-oh-wah
Only the lonely'

Tom gives a feeble impression of Roy Orbison. Having heard the song many times before, I hear Orbison's soaring voice in my head. How could I have missed this?!

The following Friday, I avoid going to the youth club where Rita and I usually meet up. I've decided to break-up with her, but don't want to do it in front of the others. Instead, I wait near her house, leaning on the gable end in a shadow cast by a flickering gaslamp. Rita comes round the corner looking a little forlorn, though she manages a wry smile when she sees me. We share a cool embrace.

'Do you want to finish?' she asks. I sigh, stumbling to find kind words.

'I want to go out with the lads, Rita. It's nothing to do with you.' I still feel tender towards her, but 'the call of the wild' is luring me away.

All You Need is Love

'Don't worry, Roy. I know how you feel. We can still be friends, can't we?' I'm relieved she's taken it so well.

'Of course we can, Rita. You know I'm still fond of you, but I want to go out having a good time with my mates.' A gentle last kiss and Rita disappears into the darkness of the back garden of her house.

* * *

I have a Valentine's card, along with a dozen red roses and a box of Cadbury's Milk Tray, delivered to Janet's house on Saturday morning. Valentine's Day is Friday, but since Janet works during the week I hold the gifts over until the Saturday. In the afternoon, calling at the house to see if my messages of love have arrived, I'm greeted not by Janet, but her mother, Edith.

'You've made a big hit there, Roy' reports a more than happy Edith. 'Janet's thrilled with the gifts, particularly the red roses, though she doesn't know what ILO VEJA NET B UCK means? Is it Latin?'

'No, it's the language of love' I reply. 'Janet will have to work it out for herself.'

Janet doesn't come downstairs. Her hair's in curlers in preparation for our night out at the Imp. When we do meet, I can see from her tender eyes that my romantic gestures have been positively and lovingly received.

* * *

I remember back to our first meeting, over a year ago, at a New Year's Eve dance at the Municipal Hall. I'm by myself, mates having gone down the Imp, which I can't afford having overspent at Christmas. There aren't many at the dance; not considered the 'In Place' to be on New Year's Eve. The décor's uninspiring with an unpolished wooden floor still showing faded badminton court markings. Decorations are sparse, with a few plastic flowers placed haphazardly on plastic tables with accompanying white plastic chairs. Round the walls are pictures of former mayors in full regalia. A three man Combo provides the music; strict tempo. Only a little rock and roll, though their rendition of *'Let's Twist Again'* isn't bad. Most of the dancers are girls, some of them from Colne Grammar School, but not

ILO VEJA NET B UCK ILO VEJA

O my luve's like a red, red rose
That's newly sprung in June
O my luve's like the melodie
That's sweetly play'd in tune

♥

TRULY,

MADLY,

DEEPLY,

IN LOVE WITH YOU!

She walks in beauty, like the night
Of cloudless climes and starry skies;
And all that's best of dark and bright
Meet in her aspect and her eyes;
Thus mellowed to that tender light
Which heaven to gaudy day denies

Your Valentine!

Mother wearing a dress designed and sewn by herself

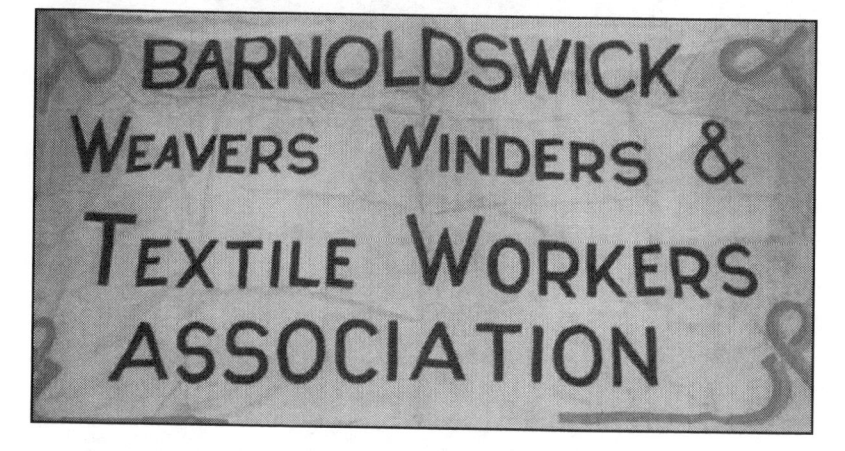

Barnoldswick Weavers Union Banner from 1920s

Father (far right) on picket-line in dispute with Qualitex Silk Company

Kershaw family in 1945 (left to right Martha, Len, Roy and Harry)

Joseph Stalin. Mother regarded him as a hero for saving the Revolution and defeating the Nazis

Burns Monument in Edinburgh. Homage paid to Rabbie Burns, Mothers favourite poet

Reluctant 2nd place in 'Bonny Child' competition, Morecambe Lido, 1949

IMPERIAL BALLROOM
NELSON

Tickets are now almost unobtainable, but a limited number of patrons will be allowed in a door. BUT PLEASE COME EARLY.

THE B.C.N. JOINT TRANSPORT HAVE PROMISED TWO LATE 'BUSES FOR BARNOLDSWICK AND EARBY.

The No. 1 Hit Paraders . . .

THE BEATLES

To-morrow (Saturday) – 7-30 to 11-30

Tickets are now almost unobtainable, but a limited number of patrons will be allowed in a door. BUT PLEASE COME EARLY.

THE B.C.N. JOINT TRANSPORT HAVE PROMISED TWO LATE 'BUSES FOR BARNOLDSWICK AND EARBY.

Doors open at 6-45 p.m.   Licensed bar open 7 p.m.

The Imperial Ballroom hosted all the top pop-groups in the late 50s and 60s

Paul Robeson addressing an anti-nuclear weapons rally in Trafalgar Square, 1959. Robeson was beloved by Mother, both for his politics and magnificent bass voice.
Source: flashbak.com/100-years-of-protesting-at-trafalgar-square-part-2-19449/

Marriage at Colne Parish Church on Halloween, 1964

Janet with Sukey, brother Len's dog

Sydney Silverman, Labour MP who brought about end of capital punishment in UK

Sharpeville Massacre in S. Africa, 1960. *Source: BBC News Photograph*

My Lai Massacre in Vietnam, 1968.
Source: US Army photographer, Ronald L. Haeberle.

I gain my BSc degree from Manchester University in 1966

Uncle Jim and family (left to right Barbara, Jim, Frank, Clarice and Jean)

Uncle Frank in 2nd World War

Woven Silk picture of Joan of Arc

all. One of the girls comes over as I sit alone at a bare table drinking my third beer out of a plastic beaker. I know Jenny has a crush on me, but I'm not interested.

'Lousy band isn't it' I quickly blurt out to forestall any offer for a dance. Jenny takes the hint, but sits down anyway. 'Who's the girl you've been dancing with over there?' I ask. 'She's not from our school, is she?'

'No, she goes to Park Secondary Modern, leaving this year' Jenny confides. 'Her name's Janet Buck. She lives next door to us, that's how I know her. If you fancy her though, you'll have to be quick. That boy in the leather jacket, Rod, is planning to ask her out.'

I'm attracted to the tall, very slim blonde; fabulous legs - just my type. I keep looking towards her, but can't work out if 'eyes across the dance floor' are reciprocated.

'Only ten minutes to midnight' announces the Combo leader. 'Better get in place to welcome in the New Year, sing *Auld Lang Syne* and give your partner a kiss.'

Everyone crowds onto the dance floor, though with the number of people there, it's hardly a crowd. I make my way over towards the attractive blonde and arms touch as we link together awaiting the midnight chimes of the Town Hall clock. Our first touch; heart beats quicker, finger tips tingle. Balloons and streamers explode from the balcony as the chimes peal out. The Combo strikes up with *Auld Lang Syne* and we all join in joyous song, moving backwards and forward as though dancing the Hokey Cokey. Everybody kisses everybody, but surely the kiss with Janet Buck lingers a little longer?

'I had the last waltz with you, two lonely people together.' The Combo continues playing, Leader crooning in an out of tune baritone voice; no Engelbert Humperdinck here. Dashing over towards my attractive blonde, I barge Rod out of the way. Neither of us is very good at the waltz, but it doesn't matter. To be in each other's arms is enough as we shuffle round the dance floor. I don't hold her too tightly and Janet demurely lowers her eyes, not meeting my own fond gaze.

'Can I walk you home?' I manage to ask, overcoming my shyness.

'Yes you can, but I'm walking up Albert Road with my friends, so you'll just have to tag along.'

Janet retrieves her coat from the cloakroom. It's a brown, fake leather coat with a fake fur collar, but there's nothing fake about my newly

All You Need is Love

found girlfriend. Despite wearing almost no makeup, her milky, translucent complexion shines through, contrasting with lightly mascara'd, olive green eyes. I wear no coat, so shiver in the icy cold night air. The walk up Albert Road is brisk, everyone trying to keep warm. Janet walks with her friends, chatting and laughing in the exciting atmosphere of the New Year. Frosty breath shimmers in the gleam of coloured lights from the Council's Christmas decorations. I walk slightly behind, joining in the conversation, but keeping a wary eye on Rod who's trying to outflank me. Janet keeps glancing in my direction so I know I'm well in.

As we approach Janet's house, down a dark, steep, cobbled back street, we peel off from the rest of the group. Holding hands seems natural. We look into each other's eyes, which also seems natural. Leaning against the gable end of a row of terraced houses I give her a gentle kiss; no more than that, not wanting to take things too far too soon.

'You've beautiful eyes' I mumble awkwardly.

'I'd better go in' responds Janet. 'My Dad'll be waiting up for me.' Is this a brush off? I follow up quickly.

'Can I see you again?'

Eyes are averted but Janet agrees to meet me outside the cinema the following Sunday. My heart leaps. Walking back home, I'm in a trance, ignoring the revellers still celebrating, singing and dancing in the main street, oblivious to cars being driven cautiously on the icy road.

'I'm the one who has most to celebrate' I joyously tell myself. 'I'm in love!'

* * *

The wait until Sunday seems an eternity. I lose what's normally a healthy appetite, so much so that Mother thinks I'm ill. 'You'd better have a spoonful of 'Emulsion' she recommends. This sickly cream coloured concoction is the family cure-all. It looks and tastes revolting, creeping out of the large bottle like slow motion vomit. I refuse to take it knowing my particular illness will not be cured by any medicine. By Sunday lunchtime I'm unable to eat at all.

Arriving at the cinema early I wait outside, leaning on the wall, hands in pockets, trying to look nonchalant. Audrey Hepburn looks down at me from a tasteful pastel-coloured poster advertising *'Breakfast at Tiffany's'*. I don't care what the film is, having other things in mind. The hand of the old fashioned wall clock clicks to Roman numeral I; it's five past seven. 'She's late' I begin to worry. 'Maybe she's not coming.' A cloying feeling begins to invade my stomach. 'Have I been stood-up?' I frown with dismay, but happily, within a few seconds my frown's replaced by an almost delirious grin. My stunning date comes round the corner, a little out of breath, wisps of hair falling over a slightly perspiring face.

'Sorry I'm late. The dog got out of the back gate and I had to chase her down the street' Janet gasps. Mental note: 'Better tell her how much I like dogs.'

The cinema's dark, trailers for next week's films having already started. The usherette flashes her torch looking for empty seats. Nothing on the back row, so we have to push past other cinema goers to reach two seats in the middle. Lack of privacy doesn't inhibit an immediate embrace and shared, long passionate kiss. We don't see much of the film though romantic strains of *'Moon River'* do filter through adding to our amorous idyll.

We remain on cloud nine over the next few weeks. Cinema Sundays; youth club Fridays. Saturday nights at the Imp to see all the top bands. Not much dancing, the floor's too packed with fans, desperate to see their heroes; The Merseyside Sound in all its glory. Sunday afternoons we go for walks, Janet with her cute Yorkshire terrier called Beauty, mine a cross Saluki and Cur named Sukey. In fact Sukey's a male, despite the name; my brother's dog, used for hunting rabbits and hares.

* * *

We take walks in the beautiful Lancashire/Yorkshire border countryside; across green, fertile agricultural land, sectioned by ancient dry stone walls. Contented cows quietly graze in the meadow until Sukey decides to gallop amongst them disturbing their peaceful munching. Sukey spots a hare in the distance and hard-wired hunting instincts kick in. Noyna, a rocky outcrop in the gentle hills, comes into view. I run ahead to scramble over the gritstone slabs with bravado, showing off in front of an unimpressed Janet. New, light grey, suede

All You Need is Love

shoes, 'borrowed' from Len, are scraped and muddied; I'll be in trouble.

Strolls by Colne Water, the river flowing gently over smooth rocks and pebbles; and to Foulridge for a stroll on the towpath of Leeds/Liverpool canal, watching and waving at decorated canal barges, maroon and green circles and triangles; green and blue arches, as relaxed crews await entrance to the 'mile tunnel'. We listen to chattering wrens, chirping sparrows and the shrill, plaintive cry of a lone kite. It's a glorious English Summer. Our favourite walk is to Wycoller, gateway to Bronte Country with Janet as my guide.

'This is where I used to live' Janet explains. 'That was our house.' She points to an old country cottage that's been expensively renovated: 'probably worth a small fortune now' I surmise.

'It wasn't like that when we were there.' Janet reads my thoughts. 'No electricity. No hot water. Nothing! The farmer even used to cut off our water supply, trying to push us out .... People say that Penelope Keith has bought a house here, but I don't know which one.'

'How did you manage?' I ask.

'I've no idea' Janet replies. 'Mum had four children to look after. Irene was still a baby and Frank a handful, always getting into scrapes and playing pranks. Dad was away working most of the time, as a painter and decorator. Even so, Mum used to run a small tea shop from the house at weekends.'

An image springs to my mind of a small girl carrying a tray of teas and currant teacakes. The girl looks terrified as she stumbles towards our small table, tray wobbling, tea spilling. Mother used to bring me to Wycoller, and we always had a snack at the mini tea shop. I look at Janet. Surely she was that small girl? I'm convinced; but Janet isn't.

We cross over the double span, ancient packhorse bridge traversing fast flowing Wycoller Beck. Walking along the river bank we come to a ruin; Wycoller Hall, built in the 16th century and used as a backdrop for Fearndean Manor in Charlotte Bronte's *Jane Eyre*.

'We used to play in the huge stone fireplace and climb on the crumbling stone walls. Frank was forever falling off, grazing his hands and shins' Janet reminisces.

* * *

Mrs Boothroyd takes us under her wing. The youth club leader, a short, dyed blondish-haired tubby woman, is beguiled by our youthful romance. Friendly eyes twinkle in an enthusiastic, ever smiling face as she persuades us to join in club activities.

'Roy, we're going to put on a show. I want you to play Sonny Boy in the song *'Climb upon my knee Sonny Boy'*. Your blond curls make you perfect for the part. It's only for fun.' I reluctantly agree.

'Climb up on my knee, Sonny Boy
Though you're only three, Sonny Boy ....'

Mrs Boothroyd's husband sings confidently in an exaggerated impression of Al Jolson whilst I, not so confidently, climb upon his knee as instructed. Wearing short trousers and knee length socks, sucking my thumb, I overcome stage fright though my acting ability isn't up to much. Everyone roars with laughter.

Our next outing's to a youth club in Burnley, to play table tennis. I somehow become captain of the table tennis team, but without corresponding skills. A whitewash by the Burnley team doesn't seem to matter as we continue to enjoy our courtship rituals. Not so enjoyable is the trip back to Colne though. Mrs Boothroyd has taken us in her old, ramshackle Ford. Her driving's erratic to say the least and, as she swerves round the many corners, furiously breaking and accelerating, I become quite nauseous. Fortunately, we arrive at our destination before I'm physically sick, Mrs Boothroyd dropping us off at the top of Janet's street. We struggle out of the car and walk gingerly down the steep pavement. Janet puts her arm around me, tenderly, lovingly, as she commiserates. 'Janet really cares for me. Janet really cares for me. Janet really cares for me' goes round and round in my head.

Another youth club trip is to Blackpool, to see Cliff Richard and the Shadows. The coach stops at 'Half Way House', a traditional stop-off point, half way to Blackpool. Mrs Boothroyd won't let us go into the pub so we sit on the bank overlooking the River Ribble. Rays of sun glint on the fast flowing water as children play at the edge trying to catch tiddlers in their small, cane handled fishing nets. We hold hands. Cliff Richard and the Shadows are appearing at the Opera House; fabulous! Cliff sings all his greatest hits: *Move It, Living Doll, Please*

All You Need is Love

Don't Tease, Fall in Love With You ……. Hank Marvin leads the Shadows with instrumentals, including *Kon Tiki*, the latest top of the charts recording. Part of the show includes a backing film of Cliff and his Group having a great time on Blackpool Pleasure Beach and other attractions in the Entertainment Capital of the West Coast. We fall into a contented, blissful sleep on the long journey home.

* * *

'Had a great time at Thornton Manor Jazz Club last week.' Tom's in full voice, competing with the crowd of boisterous, rowdy youths in the public bar of the Crown Hotel. 'You're missing all the best nights out, Curly.' (Curly has become my new nickname, much to my annoyance).
'Going to be a big party at Pendle Inn next Friday. Why don't you come?' adds Ian.
'He can't' jeers Al. 'He's under't thumb we' 'is woman.' Others join in, mocking mercilessly. 'No more good times for you.' I feel under pressure – ridiculed.
'It's your round, Curly.' Finishing a pint, I push my way to the chaotic bar, customers loudly sharing their news. 'Burnley won three nil today'; 'Picked up a fantastic girl last night, a real goer'; 'Cliff Richard was on Six Five Special.' Random reminders of carefree lifestyles crowd in as I'm joined by Al to help carry brimming pint glasses of beer. No short measures in this pub. 'Five pints of Red Barrel, please, Glenda' I shout to the busy, flustered bar maid. Al continues taunting me with stories of alcohol fuelled adventures
'Thinking of packing her in tonight' I bogusly claim, trying to reconstruct an image of a devil may care free spirit, playing the field. In the confusion I fail to notice Rod, my rival for Janet's affections, leaning on the bar next to us.
After another pint, we leave the Crown to catch the Nelson bus. The Tornados are playing down the Imp, currently at number one with *'Telstar'*. I'm to meet Janet there, but arriving on the dance floor, I've a gut wrenching shock. Rod's dancing energetically with Janet who, though seeing me, avoids eye contact. Jealousy wells up. I'm frozen to the spot despite the heat emanating from vigorous dancers.
'Don't worry about her, Roy. She's with Rod now. He told Janet what you said at the Crown.'

Ola Borowski grabs my arm and pulls me onto the dance floor. She's been chasing me for ages, but I've had eyes only for Janet. In any case, Ola's short and slim with jet black hair and, though quite pretty, not my type at all.

'We're having a party at my house tonight. Parents away so we'll have a great time. Everybody's coming.'

After a couple of dances I disconsolately exit to drown my sorrows at the bar. The dance is coming to an end when Ola pulls me off the bar stool to join the babbling, joyous group leaving to catch the last bus to Colne.

'Come on, Roy, don't mope, there's plenty to drink at my house.'

By now the beer's eliciting a response to Ola's advances and on reaching the Party house I'm in a brighter, more amorous mood. She leads me into one of the bedrooms and we dive onto the coat strewn bed, though our passionate, gymnastic wrestling is soon brought to an end as other couples drunkenly crash into the room. We go back downstairs where music's still playing, by now slow and smoochy.

'You ask how long I'll love you;
I'll tell you true.
Until the twelfth of never,
I'll still be loving you.'

Johnny Mathis' silky voice croons the romantic ballad as couples cling to each other, mimicking Lena Horne's *'New Fangled Tango'*; 'Just like romancing while dancin' ...... who's dancin'? We join them, but I soon slump onto the sofa, exhausted.

Jenny drifts over and sits on the sofa arm to whisper in my ear.

'Look out of the window, Roy.'

Through an inebriated haze I see Janet gliding down the drive away from the house. Jumping up, I dash to the door and hurry after her, leaving my coat behind, ignoring the frosty night air. Janet looks vulnerable under the illuminating light of a street lamp. We walk slowly together for some time, neither speaking nor looking at each other.

'Didn't make much of the Tornadoes' I murmur to break the silence.

'No, not as good as other groups we've seen' she perfunctorily agrees. We fall back into silence.

All You Need is Love

On reaching the gable end of Janet's house I reach out for a hug, but she pulls away.

'Shall we go to the pictures tomorrow?' I nervously ask.

'No, I'm washing my hair' comes the abrupt reply. I slink away into the dark, unforgiving night, quietly sobbing.

* * *

A few weeks later I'm again at the Imp, this time sat on a bar stool rather than dancing. Girls ask me to dance, but I decline.

'Another pint please, Frank.' The barman's an old school friend of mine. 'Not many people down tonight.'

'No, they haven't booked a top line act; only a local Group, the Dolphins. Most of the girls are here to see Tony Hicks the lead guitarist. He's leaving soon to join The Hollies in Manchester. Can't you hear them all screaming?' I'm not interested.

Out of the corner of my eye I see Jenny coming towards me. 'Oh, no, she's going to ask me to dance'. I turn to chat to Frank again; I'm such a cad!

'You can't avoid me so easily, Roy' Jenny scolds. She seems in a happy but thoughtful mood. 'I've got some good news for you. I was at Rabanos last night with friends.' She pauses. 'Including Janet.' My heart skips a beat. 'She was in tears, saying how much she misses you. Janet really cares for you, Roy. Do you want to go out with her again?' For a moment I'm speechless but manage to blurt out 'Of course I do!' Jenny looks somewhat crestfallen, but her expression quickly turns to an understanding smile.

'She'll see you at the Grand in Nelson tomorrow night at seven.'

'Thanks, Jenny.' I give her a hug and kiss on the cheek. 'I really appreciate what you've done for me.' We look at each other. There's a little sadness in our eyes.

The next day I walk around in a trance. Unable to eat, feeling sick, constantly looking at my watch. It must be love. We're both on time for our reconciliatory date. Looking into each other's eyes, embracing and kissing passionately, we've no idea what film is showing, and don't care. 'Making up's definitely better than breaking up' I conclude. We resume our pre-breakup routine; cinema dates, walks on the canal and in the countryside, trips out with the youth club, dancing down the Imp, listening to pop music. Everything's even better than before. One pop song seems particularly apposite, by the Dubliners.

> 'I met my love, by the gas works wall.
> Dreamed a dream, by the old canal.
> Kissed my girl, by the factory wall.
> Dirty old town, dirty old town.'

It's a bit unfair to describe Colne as a dirty old town, though there is a gasworks near a working-man's club we frequent. Certainly dreams are dreamt by Foulridge canal. Janet's just started work at a weaving mill, so when I go to meet her at the end of her shift, we kiss by the cotton shed wall.

* * *

'It won't last' Mother confides to Aunty Mary. 'Roy's going to University in September. He'll soon forget about her. She's only a mill girl.'

The speciousness of the overheard conversation arouses my ire. After all, most of my Mother's working life has been spent as 'a mill girl'. She's always preached that 'everyone's equal' and championed the virtues of the working class. Clearly some are more equal than others in her eyes. I burst into the living room from the kitchen to upbraid Mother for her insensitive, obdurate remarks. A startled silence follows, though, deep down, unwanted doubts begin to gnaw.

Doubts that resurface as I watch an Alun Owen play on ITV's Armchair Theatre, *Lena, O My Lena*, the story of a sensitive university student, Tom, who gets a temporary job on a loading dock in a Lancashire factory. He's smitten with Lena, a girl working in a machine shop next door, played by Billie Whitelaw. Lena responds to his affections though she's already dating Glyn, an uncouth, bullying forklift truck driver, more brawn than brains, claiming her for himself. It ends up in a fight between the two suitors with Tom taking quite a beating.

'Why did you get into a fight with him, Tom? You were always going to lose.' Lena tries to console him, tenderly wiping away blood from

All You Need is Love

his battered face.

'I'm fond of you, Lena. I can't stand seeing you kiss that moron; you're too good for him.' Lena strokes Tom's bruised hands and gently whispers to him.

'But Tom, you must know there's no future for us. We live in different worlds. You'll be going back to university in a few weeks and there's no way we can continue seeing each other. In your heart of hearts you must know this.' Tom begins to sob.

'But I love you, Lena.' She gently kisses him.

'No, you don't love me, it's only infatuation. Go back to university and find someone else to love. In any case my life's here with Glyn. He's rough and ready but we've known each other since childhood, living on the same street, going to the same school. I know where I stand with him.'

The Play ends with Lena walking back to a nervous Glyn as all is forgiven in a warm, loving embrace. A despairing Tom walks out of the job, and out of Lena's life.

Coronation Street's one of my much-liked TV programmes, Ken Barlow an admired character. Ken returns from Manchester University to his working-class roots in Weatherfield, where he marries Valerie Tatlock, daughter of a near neighbour. Ken takes a job as a teacher in the local secondary modern school. 'So it can work' I convince myself.

My so-called mates continue to ridicule me and even Len tries to break up the relationship. 'Don't be a fool, Roy. Go away to university and have a good time or you'll regret it.'

My mind continues in turmoil.

* * *

Over the next few months Janet and I grow closer, seeing each other several times a week. Sexual tensions increase, relieved only by frequent masturbation; but even then powerful desires refuse to subside. Testosterone fuelled mates relate stories of their sexual exploits. 'I'm being left behind in this age of free love' I tell myself. Plucking up courage, I go to the chemists. 'A packet of …….. Aspros, please.' I bottle it, but try again. 'A packet of ….. indigestion tablets, please.' I bottle it again. 'You want condoms?' asks the chemist, with a knowing smile. 'Yes, packet of three.' Back at home I try putting on the rubber sheath. It's a struggle, but I finally manage it.

As I'm leaving Janet's house one evening, I take her in my arms for a goodnight kiss. 'Look in my top pocket, Janet. Do you like what you see?' I ask. She pulls out the condom, blushing and looking acutely embarrassed. 'You can have sex without love, but you can't love someone without wanting sex.' I mumble pre-prepared lines, but they don't sound as convincing as when I'd practiced at home. Janet remains silent, quickly replacing the condom, though an especially sensual kiss makes me believe there's more to come.

A few weeks later we're walking back to Janet's house after watching Dr No at the cinema. The erotic emergence of Ursula Andress from foaming waves is still fixed in my mind and overheated imagination.

'Everybody's out on Saturday if you want to come round. Mum, Dad and Irene are going to Morecambe on the motorbike and sidecar' Janet whispers in a matter of fact voice, though I detect hidden meaning. Is this going to be the day I lose my virginity?

Arriving at the house early Saturday afternoon, Janet opens the door before I knock, having watched for me through the kitchen window. She's wearing her front buttoned, figure hugging, striped yellow and green shift dress. I'm bewitched and breathless. Taking me by the hand, she leads me up the stairs to her small, single bed room and closes the curtain. We're both nervous and embarrassed, clumsily undressing in restricted space. Janet unbuttons her dress revealing a white bra which I nervously unfasten, hands shaking. She slips under the single sheet on the bed as I sit on the edge, trying, with some difficulty, to put on a condom. Climbing into the bed, I immediately caress Janet's soft, unblemished body. Firm, pointed breasts are all I've dreamt of. I kiss the nipples, which harden to my touch. Intercourse isn't so easy, our inexperience and lack of room in the bed making it difficult to assume positions I've read about in a much-thumbed copy of Lady Chatterley's Lover. 'Search for the clitoris had been the advice from Mick, the town stud. But I don't know what to look for so, in frustration, revert to animal-like penetration. Intercourse lasts only a short while and a feeling of ecstasy is followed by deep relief. Janet's quiet sigh hints at a similar response. We've done it. We're now part of

All You Need is Love

the sexual revolution!

Over the next few weeks we become increasingly passionate, taking every opportunity to make love. On the couch late at night after Janet's parents have gone to bed. Even in a small shed at the top of the street. On the back seat of Len's Rover 60 car's another uncomfortable setting, parking in various 'lover's lanes' out in the wooded countryside.

We go on holiday to the caravan in Bolton-le-Sands, chaperoned by Cousin Barbara and her husband Eric; though not very effectively. Driving Len's Rover into Morecambe, we visit Janet's parents and sister Irene, on holiday in a tiny two room holiday flatlet. Granville's bought his two daughters new coats from the outdoor market, fake leopard-print; black and white for Irene, beige and yellow for Janet. In the evening I escort the glamorous sisters to a dance on the North Pier, the Joe Loss Orchestra providing the music. My chest swells with pride as I walk along the prom, arm in arm with two fur coated, sensational blondes. We enter the dance hall to the sound of *'In the Mood'*, Joe Loss energetically conducting his famous orchestra. I spend the evening fighting off many suitors for Irene, who's still only fifteen.

A visit to *Gypsy Rose Lee*, who examines my hand, looking intently for clues to the future. 'You'll never do manual work for a living' she wails. Since my hands are smooth and white, this doesn't seem a particularly perceptive revelation. Janet laughs. But she doesn't laugh at the next prediction. 'You'll travel the world.' Neither of us can understand what this means as we've no plans to travel further than Lancashire.

* * *

I leave for the University in Manchester, staying in Chorlton-cum-Hardy digs with two grammar school friends. Janet phones through the week and I return home every weekend, the desire to see Janet overwhelming the attractions of University life. Condoms no longer play any part in our coitus; ardour too impatient. The inevitable happens.

'Roy, I've something to tell you. Dad took me to the doctors last week saying I looked pale and anaemic. The doctor said I was anaemic; but also pregnant!' I take Janet's hand to console her; she looks devastated.

'Don't worry, love, we can get married. I'll get a part-time job while I'm at University. Together with my grant, we'll have enough to live on.'

My main worry is how to tell Mother. Walking back home I push open the gate; but my courage fails me and I carry on walking. This happens several times before I finally manage to climb the steps and quietly enter the house. Mother's dusting the piano, busy as usual.

'Janet's having a baby' I stammer. A look of total shock disfigures a face drained of blood. She collapses into the chair.

'I knew it. I knew it. Her parents shouldn't have let you stay so late every week. You'll have to leave University now and get married. Your life's ruined!'

Neither is Father happy, though he takes it more in his stride.

'What's done is done.' He goes to see Janet's parents.

'You shouldn't have left them alone on Saturday nights.' Father admonishes Granville, as instructed by Mother.

'You shouldn't have let them go to Morecambe' comes the retaliatory response.

They leave it at that, agreeing to share wedding costs.

'They can live with us when they're married, we have a spare bedroom. It won't cost them anything so Roy can continue at University' offers Granville. Father nods in agreement, grateful Janet's parents are being so understanding.

We go to see the Vicar at Colne Parish Church, and since neither of us has been confirmed, attending church only occasionally, the interview's a little fraught. There's no explanation as to why we want to get married in church, except 'it's the done thing'. The Vicar's not at all impressed, but gives us a brief sermon on the importance of marriage and joining the family of God. We promise to attend church more often in future.

'I suppose you want to get married as soon as possible in the circumstances' suggests the Vicar. 'There's only one date available in the next month; the 31st October. Nobody wants to marry on Halloween.'

It doesn't make any difference to us, so we agree the date. Other than having yet to face the ironic laughter of my mates, everything is done and dusted and I can now concentrate on catching up with my university work.

* * *

The phone rings in the lobby of Mrs Rigby's house in Chorlton-cum-Hardy, our Manchester digs. I dash to the phone expecting it to be Janet, but it isn't. Instead, it's the quiet, subdued voice of Granville, Janet's Dad.

'You don't have to worry, but Janet's in hospital. She's had a miscarriage.' I take a deep breath. 'She's OK, but very upset.' Granville continues with a note of resignation. 'You'd better come home tomorrow, we'll visit her in hospital; she's in Marsden.'

'Thanks for letting me know' I mumble inanely, short of breath. 'I'll come on the afternoon bus.'

Visiting hours are seven to eight in the evening. Granville, Edith and I wait for the door to open, not speaking, glum faces. Janet's at the far end of the ward and Granville walks swiftly to the bed, me in his wake. She's always been 'Dad's girl'. Parents give her a hug whilst I remain in the background feeling nervous, and somehow guilty. They move away and I shuffle forward to give Janet a kiss, taking her hand.

'I'm so sorry, Roy. I fell at the bottom of the stairs, it all started from there.'

Trying to put on an air of acceptance and bravado, which I don't feel, I whisper: 'No need to worry love, it's my fault, not yours. I'll look after you.' Our eyes are full of love and forgiveness.

Back home I break the news to Mother. Despite her brusque and uncompromising demeanour, Mother's compassionate; like Ena Sharples on Coronation Street. She's the first one family members turn to when things go wrong. Having lost her first baby when he was five months old, she understands the agony Janet's going through. Nevertheless, she can't resist.

'Are you still going to get married? You don't need to.' I don't reply.

On Friday Janet's discharged from Marsden, returning to her Peter Street home. In the evening I walk down to the house, mind still in ferment. What am I going to say? How will Janet feel? Slowly opening the back yard gate I knock on the door though in fact it's ajar, so I enter the kitchen. Granville's in the living room, still very subdued.

'Janet's in bed resting. You'd better go up.'

I silently climb the narrow stairs, anxious, still not knowing what to say. Sitting on a low stool next to the bed, I gently take Janet's hand.

'How are you feeling, love. Is there any pain?' She doesn't reply, her face and lips contorted as though about to weep. I hold her hand more tightly.

'Do you still want to get married?' Janet's words tumble out breathlessly. I lean over to hug her, kissing her furrowed brow. Our faces almost touch as we look deeply into each other's eyes.

'Of course I do.'

The low-key wedding takes place on Saturday 31st October 1964, Janet wearing sister-in-law Maureen's wedding dress. Janet's 18, I'm 20. We're both nervous throughout the ceremony and wedding lunch and I spill the wine whilst making my speech, hands trembling. It's with relief when we leave the Reception, again in Len's car. 'Honeymoon on the West Coast' reports the *Colne Times*.

CHAPTER 6

Don't Drink and Drive!

Mother shouts up the stairs: 'Roy, Roy, your Uncle Lloyd says he'll give you a job during the school holidays.'
I sense some reservation in her voice. Lloyd's the blackest sheep of the family; a heavy drinking, womanising, fist-fighting builder who's led his wife, Aunty Mary, a merry dance. But needs must, so Mother swallows her doubts in the cause of my pecuniary plight. The job's as labourer with his small family building firm which consists of himself, son Harvey, nephew Keith and a family friend, Mick. Mother insists I 'tip up' my wages and she'll give me spending money, though on hearing this, Lloyd takes me to one side.
'I'll tell Martha I'm paying you £10 a week, but will give you £12. I know the cost of a pint these days.'
Lloyd's firm has built up a reputation for building 'shippens' (cowsheds) on dairy and sheep farms in the area and I'll be working on an upland hill farm near Malham in the Yorkshire Dales. Malham Tarn and Cove are popular beauty spots amid rolling hills and rugged moorland where we've had many walks alongside Gordale Beck to the spectacular Waterfalls. Surrounded by lush grass and ancient trees, the imposing cliffs of Gordale Scar are passed on the way to the quiet expanse of Malham Tarn. Cries of moorhens, coots and teal often pierce the peaceful scene as they flutter in the reed beds or take wing in blue skies on warm, sunny days. Though I won't be admiring any of this scenery, or basking in sunshine, as I assume builder's labourer duties.
It's six o'clock on a July morning and the sun's already beginning to warm the damp air as I wait at the side of the road, wearing baggy trousers – too big for me – found by Mother at a jumble sale. A denim shirt's also too big, purchased from the same source. Trousers are, just about, held up by a frayed leather belt. Old, steel-toed boots have been provided by Lloyd, their well worn, scruffy appearance adding to the

image of a down at heel Irish navvy, as I step into my new role. A clanging, screeching sound precedes the appearance of a rackety, ancient vehicle. It's an old Commer post office van with side windows boarded up, dark green bodywork rusting, and tyres almost threadbare. Lloyd's driving the van, which pulls up jerkily at the kerbside.

'Get in the back' he shouts jovially as he looks, much amused, at my get up. 'You certainly look the part. Bit different from your school uniform.'

I struggle to open the back door, eventually managing, though without help from unsympathetic passengers. A sullen atmosphere pervades with Harvey and Mick smoking, filling the space with a murky grimness. All three sit on cement bags down the sides of the van where I join them. No welcoming 'good morning'. Harvey in particular looks morose, clearly having a hangover from what must have been a big night out. Keith's trying, unsuccessfully, to doze. Lloyd's an unconventional, nay reckless, driver, swerving and speeding through narrow country lanes without any concern for other road users, or his passengers. We're regularly thrown from side to side, colliding with spades, hods and other building equipment thrown into the back of the van.

'Slow down you silly bugger' shouts Harvey to his father, but Lloyd takes no notice. It's that sort of relationship.

I feel depressed and nauseous. 'What have I let myself in for?' I morbidly ask myself.

'Instruction' in the art of builder's labourer is by trial and error. I'm to be hod and breeze block carrier; mixer man, shovelling sand, cement and hardcore into an antiquated concrete mixer; dumper driver, chugging concrete and building materials around the site. Hands are cut and bruised until Lloyd finds me a tatty pair of leather gloves. Bricks regularly fall out of the damaged hod and I drop breeze blocks from my weak, soft 'academic' hands; thank goodness for steel-toed boots. The dumper has to be hand cranked using a starting handle, engine often kicking back causing further bruising of forearms and shins. The exhaust chimney spews out thick, black diesel fumes, directly into the face of the unfortunate dumper driver; me, usually. I struggle through the first week, hating the job but thinking about cash rewards.

TGIF – 'Thank God it's Friday' is the labourer's hymn. I'll receive

Don't Drink and Drive!

my first pay packet and have a date with Janet so lots to look forward to? It doesn't work out that way.

Breeze blocks are piled in the farm yard, next to the sheep dip where I've to climb up the soaring stack to take blocks from the summit. Two at a time is standard, but they're too heavy for me, so usually I carry just one, much chided by Keith and Mick. Resolving to lift two, I scramble up the tower of breeze blocks and hug a pair to my chest. Climbing down has to be backwards; no room to turn at the top. Slowly and carefully I descend the 'mountain', successfully until the last row of blocks. One of them tips as I stretch towards 'terra firma', throwing me backwards. Two steps and I enter an unknown world of stars, flashing lights and a blood curdling scream as I fall into the sheep dip, sinking to my haunches. Pushing to the surface, I'm greeted not by concerned fellow workers but by a posse of unsympathetic morons shouting and jeering with great hilarity.

'If you've dropped any breeze blocks in there, you'd better dive down and recover them' orders Lloyd.

We finish work at six o'clock. By now I've dried out, though still smelling strongly of disinfectant and covered in sheep hairs. My first wage packet softens the blow as I clamber into the back of the van, now sitting with Keith who's befriended me. I look forward to getting home, having a bath and taking Janet to the cinema. The van speeds along as usual, but I don't mind since the faster it goes, the sooner I'll be home. Suddenly the Commer swerves, not on a bend, but into the car park of a pub; ironically the *Woolly Sheep Inn* near Skipton. Neither Keith nor I are impressed, both wanting to get back home quickly to see our girlfriends. We traipse into the public bar where Harvey orders a round of drinks; pints of *Black Sheep Yorkshire Beer*, adding insult to injury. I'm no longer at ease with sheep related liquids. They're downed in one by Harvey and Mick, who orders another round. Keith looks at me in dismay as he knows from past experience these Friday night sessions can go on for a long time. We can't keep up with the heavy drinkers, but still manage to down a couple of pints of the strong ale in quick time, instilling us with a sense of bravado. Keith manages to pocket the van keys, which Lloyd's left on the bar table. He gives me a wink and nods towards the pub exit and we surreptitiously shuffle to the door, heading towards the car park. Keith jumps into the driving seat, inserts the ignition key and tries to start the van. No response. He rattles the long gear stick, depresses the clutch and tries again in desperation. Still no response. We drift back into the pub where another two pints of *Black Sheep Beer* await. Lloyd has a knowing smirk on his face. He's not conned so easily.

It's after nine o'clock when we eventually leave and at first I see the funny side of the situation, laughing at the raucous, alcohol inspired jokes and humour. But soon foreboding takes over. I can't go home in this state; it'd mean the end of my job and confirm Mother's worst opinions of Lloyd.

'Lloyd, I can't go home like this' I shout above the din. 'You'll have to drop me off at the top of Skipton Road.'

'You'll be OK. You've not had that much to drink' is Lloyd's unhelpful reply. In his terms, that's probably true; in my terms it's only marginally true; in Mother's terms it's totally untrue.

'You'd better ring Martha up when you get home. Tell her we've had to work late and that I'm staying at your house tonight' I plead.

I don't know whether my message has got through with all the pandemonium in the van, though I am dropped off at the top of Skipton Road as requested, so keep my fingers crossed. Wobbling down the street towards Janet's house, I try thinking up excuses, but without success so I decide to throw myself at the mercy of Janet's dad, Granville. Janet has two older brothers, Frank and Granville, who've been known to drink to excess on occasions so hope that Granville senior might have a more understanding view of my predicament than my own parents.

I push through the gate into the back yard and knock on the kitchen door. All the lights are on in the house. Granville cautiously opens the door, face both bemused and wary, not knowing who this late evening visitor is.

'Can you help me?' is my feeble, whispered supplication.

'You'd better come in' Granville says in a half concerned, half laughing voice. 'Janet's gone to bed. She's not happy.'

I rush to the kitchen sink, where much of the *Black Sheep Beer* returns with a vengeance.

'You'd better sleep on the couch, but not in those filthy, stinking rags. And take off the boots, you look like you've walked through a muddy farmyard' (which I have).

Granville goes upstairs, returning with oversize pyjamas. I can hear

Don't Drink and Drive!

laughter and chortling, including Janet's voice; but she stays put.

* * *

It's Friday night and I'm to meet up with my mates at the Commercial Pub at the top of Skipton Road. Though most of us are not yet 18, the publican turns a blind eye; a don't ask, don't tell policy. I put on my Italian suit and winkle-picker shoes, the latest fashion. Mother looks suspicious.

'Where are you going?' she asks. 'You better not be drinking.'

Mother's heard rumours I'm associating with Jack Brown who's known to drink, smoke and go out with girls; though she's no proof.

'I'm going to meet my mates at Rabanos. Then we're going to the flicks' is my less than truthful reply.

Rabanos is a new coffee bar located across from the Commercial Hotel. It's the 'In Place' for the 'In Crowd' where teenagers meet to gossip and play the latest records on a state of the art Juke Box. *Elvis Presley*, *Everly Brothers*, *Brenda Lee*, *Connie Francis* and *Del Shannon* are the most frequently played records. For the price of a cup of coffee we can sit there most of the evening listening to maximum decibel pop music. A high tech coffee machine spits and splutters, seeming at times to almost explode as clouds of steam envelop the equipment. Smoking's allowed and dirty jokes abound. As a non-smoker, and unable to understand half the jokes, I'm on the fringe, but still manage to join in, laughing in the right places.

At the Commercial the evening's merriment begins. 'Mine's a pint of bitter' shouts Jack. 'Same for me' adds Dave, my best friend from grammar school. My round, and with three more mates arriving, it's expensive. I tot up the money in my pocket; sixpence short.

'Lend me a bob, will you?' I whisper to Nick who left secondary school at 15 and has a job at his father's garage. He's flush.

'OK, but you still owe me sixpence from last week.'

'Just started a Sunday morning pareround. I'll pay you back everything next week' I assure him.

We sit in the corner of the noisy, smoke filled public bar where Paddy entertains us with exaggerated stories of his latest 'conquests'. Nobody believes him, but I listen intently to pick up tips on 'how to seduce girls'. To date I've had little success, though, of course, never admit it.

My only 'French Letter' lies dormant in my wallet.

'I'm going over to Rabanos to see my girlfriend' I announce, pushing my way through the crowded bar. 'Get me a pint of mild in, I won't be long. Just going to fix up a date at the cinema for tomorrow.'

In my absence, an older woman with an angry, disdainful look on her face comes into the bar. Looking round distastefully, her sharp eyes spot Jack Brown drinking and smoking in a dark corner. Other drinkers move out of her way as she forcefully strides towards the den of iniquity.

'Where's our Roy?' she demands to know of the jovial bunch of revellers. 'I know he came in here because Mrs Watson told me.'

A hush comes over the pub bar and for a few seconds the gang looks at her in startled silence. But Jack, mind working at a furious pace, soon comes out with a devastating response.

'He's gone over to Rabanos with his woman to buy some more fags. He'll be back soon. We've got another pint waiting for him.'

* * *

'Here's a gin and orange' whispers Lloyd as he hands me a glass. 'I've put a lot of orange in it so your Mother'll think it's cordial, but there's a double in there as well. I can see her keeping a close eye on you.'

I drink the sickly sweet concoction trying to lift my mood and avoid boring conversations with maiden aunts.

We're in the bar of a hotel in Bootle, at the Reception for my brother Len's wedding to Maureen, a Liverpool girl. There's lots of chatter and laughter, most of it coming from the bride's family, with little intermingling; the norm on such occasions in Lancashire. Our family's a little subdued, not many smiles except in Lloyd's corner of the bar. There's also a preponderance of females lacking male escorts. I know the reason for the long faces, my own low spirits and the paucity of men, remembering the delayed shock when date and time of the wedding had been announced.

> **Mr and Mrs John Stinson**
>
> Request the honour of your presence
> at the marriage of their daughter
>
> Maureen to
> Mr Leonard Kershaw
>
> at Litherland Parish Church
> on Saturday, fifth May, 1962 at three o'clock

At first the date and time hadn't caused anxiety since a Saturday afternoon wedding in May isn't unusual. But when Burnley win the FA Cup semi-final against Fulham at the beginning of April, I look again at the invitation with a cold shiver. The Cup Final is to be on Saturday, 5th May at three o'clock! This is the first time Burnley had reached the final since 1947, losing 1 - 0 to Charlton Athletic. Most of my family, including me, being big fans of our local club, are put decidedly between the proverbial 'rock and a hard place'. Even the Stinsons, ardent football fans themselves, won't be happy at missing the Final, even though their own team 'The Toffees' isn't involved. Several uncles and cousins have RSVP'd to say they aren't able to come to the wedding, using feeble excuses that everyone knows are lies. Of course, I'm not able to decline, under pain of death from both Mother and Brother.

'We are gathered here together to celebrate the very special love ………,'
The Vicar opens the ceremony in a broad Scouse accent. Almost inaudibly from the back of the Church, comes the cheering of ecstatic fans as two teams run onto hallowed Wembley turf. One of my uncles has brought a transistor radio.

At the Reception, gloom hangs like a cloud Burnley having lost 3 - 1 to their hated rivals, Tottenham Hotspur, Jimmy Greaves once again proving Burnley's nemesis. The hotel bar's doing good business as despondent Burnley fans drown their sorrows with pints of Threlfalls Bitter. Lloyd continues providing me with fortified orange cordial, so by the time the coach arrives to take the Kershaw contingent back home, everyone's quite drunk, including me. Luckily, though, I'm not the centre of attention as Len's best man, Joseph (a handsome, curly haired young farmer) is in a worse state than anyone. He has to be carried onto the coach, where he's looked after by his blonde, beautiful fiancée. She's clearly reluctant in this role, showing great distaste as she pats his sweaty forehead with serviettes from the hotel. It passes through my mind that this particular engagement might not result in marriage.

* * *

We arrive at Sunnyside Boarding House in Blackpool; cheapest in town. There are eight of us, all teenagers, mostly from 'The Saints' football team which I play for. A matronly landlady looks dismayed as she opens the creaking front door. 'Another set of louts' her eyes seem to say, though it's too late now; she's already taken the booking.

'No smoking, drinking or girls in the rooms' warns the landlady in a strict, Scottish accent. 'And no eating your own food, especially fish and chips. They stink the house out' she continues. 'Breakfast's between eight and nine, and evening meal at seven o'clock, prompt. The front door's locked at midnight and don't make any noise when you come in. We do have *other* guests.'

Printed instructions decorate the entrance hall: 'All breakages must be paid for'; 'Don't bring sand in from the beach'; 'Telephone only to be used in an emergency'. A regular home from home.

We've been allocated two rooms. A double bunk and king-sized bed have been squeezed into a space normally suitable for one standard double bed. There's a sink in the corner, but nothing else. The view from the single, wooden framed sash window is of a high brick wall, covered with graffiti. I fling my small, battered suitcase onto the top bunk but, despite grim surroundings, I'm not downhearted. I'm here for a week of freedom from watchful eyes of an overprotective Mother; a week of freedom to drink, smoke and find fun-loving girls. I still can't quite believe I've been allowed this escapade, and that my parents have agreed to foot the bill. No doubt Father's influence.

Don't Drink and Drive!

The evening meal gives a taste of things to come. Only five of us are there, the other three can't wait to sample Blackpool night life; the affluent ones who've left school and started work. Watery soup is of indeterminate flavour, though odd floating globules of pink mush indicate tomato. This is followed by bangers and mash, onion sauce and baked beans, with thick, curdled gravy. Sausages are overcooked, some would say burnt. Mashed potatoes are undercooked with lumps of almost raw potato. A minute cube of bright yellow sponge cake, with thin yet lumpy custard, finishes the meal. Portions are small and lukewarm, but we don't complain. We're not here for culinary pleasures.

Only four of us turn up for breakfast the next morning. The three 'out on the town' revellers are already suffering hangovers and the other missing teenager is just too lazy to get up. Breakfast matches the evening meal with one runny, undercooked fried egg and a single slice of charred streaky bacon. Thick slices of toast. How can toast that's so burnt be so cold? Only weak tea's served, no coffee.

By mid-morning the full team manages to congregate, agreeing to go to a coffee bar someone's spotted down a narrow street near the promenade. I'm wearing flared, light grey and blue checked trousers with a figure hugging flowered shirt and oversized collar. Footwear's a pair of moccasin style light brown slip-on loafers, largely hidden by the flapping, wide trousers. Malcolm has on tight, powder blue jeans, which I'm envious of; keep asking if I can borrow them. Most of the others wear Levi style blue jeans and red shirts; almost a uniform.

We go into a tobacco shop to buy cigarettes. Some buy Players or Woodbines, but I purchase Passing Clouds brand. They're more expensive, but classy and oval shaped: 'For a sophisticated taste' says the advertising poster. The others chide me.

'Why've you bought those pansy cigarettes?' scoffs Tom. 'You don't smoke properly, don't even swallow.' This is true, but I stick to my image of a sophisticated partaker of superior tobacco.

The Cavern Coffee Bar lives up to or, more accurately, down to its name as we descend steep steps into a dark, mysterious basement, lit only by dim sidelights. The smoky atmosphere's accentuated by clouds of vapour from two coffee machines. *Apache* by The Shadows plays loudly on a large, ornate Juke Box. We buy coffees and light up. How Cool!

Coming out into bright sunshine, all the brighter having exited the dark Cavern, I put on my sexy 'Hollywood' sunglasses 'borrowed' from brother Len. We walk along the bustling promenade where families with small children carrying buckets and spades, as well as long canes with small nets, have their hands full. Parents wear colourful, wide-brimmed hats. A smiling woman with dyed blonde hair, bright red lipstick, wearing denim shorts that are too small, low cut blouse exposing red, sunburnt breasts. 'Mutton dressed as lamb' Mother would have said, 'middle age trying to recapture youth.' She's accompanied by a younger man wearing a joke bow tie, which lights up every time he turns his head. Groups of trousered young girls with 'kiss me quick' hats on; raucous youths in shorts and flip-flops; older couples, the men wearing suit and tie, women in long-sleeved flowery dresses, fastened to the neck.

'See Stella in the Palace of Strange Girls. The Show they tried to stop!' screams a large, flashy poster. A glimpse of Stella, but no more. 'Come in, boys, you'll be shocked. It was her father's fault' shouts a care-worn wrinkled face, in a falsely enthusiastic voice. *'The Zebra Man'* is another *'unmissable'* attraction, as is *'The Bearded Lady'*. *'Samson, Man of Iron. The Strongest Man in the World'* offers cash to anyone who can challenge him. Rocky, our gang's 'hardman', pushes forward, but we persuade him against. Continuing along the prom, I buy shrimps from a seafood stall, whilst others purchase ice creams from famous *'Pablo's Ice Cream Parlour'*. For lunch we have fish & chips wrapped in the *Blackpool Gazette*. The sound of George Formby singing *'My Little Stick of Blackpool Rock'* accompanies a quick visit to a small rock making plant. Flicking through postcards for sale in a seafront stall, I try to find one suitable for sending home, but most of them are saucy – sexy, leggy women with big bums and big boobs; downtrodden male companions. One shows a honeymoon couple leaving a hotel, 'The Halfway Inn'. 'They must have named it after you!' a disappointed new bride says scornfully. I settle for a scene of Blackpool Tower and trams floating down the sea front.

We go into the Penny Arcade to try our luck on the slot machines. Only two cherries, not three, on the one-armed bandit. Pennies are stacked on the edge, but don't fall over the 'tipping point' on another tempting machine. A mini-crane grips a small teddy bear, but releases it prematurely. We exit with lighter pockets, but at least we've heard

Don't Drink and Drive!

some of the latest records; *'Runaway'* by Del Shannon; *'Calendar Girl'* by Neil Sedaka. At the entrance to the South Pier big posters advertise Stars appearing at various entertainment venues in town. Arthur Askey and Kathy Kirby on the North Pier; Ken Dodd and Joseph Locke at the Opera House; Hilda Baker with Don Lang and his Frantic Five are appearing on the South Pier. But the Show that attracts us most is at the Winter Gardens where Adam Faith, John Barry Seven and Emile Ford and the Checkmates are on stage. We book for the Matinee on Thursday, the only seats available.

As little time as possible is spent in the boarding house as the room's become increasingly smelly. Though smoking's not allowed, we do it anyway. Personal hygiene doesn't seem of importance, the smell of stale sweat permeating the environment. Farting's almost compulsory. One particularly obnoxious roommate insists on masturbating. 'Fourth time' he triumphantly informs us.

Though drinking and smoking continue at a hectic pace, success with females is limited. I manage to pick up a girl in the Tower Ballroom, buying her rum and cokes much of the evening. We do have a few dances, *'The Twist'* being all the rage, but it begins to dawn on me it's the girl who's picked me up, not vice-versa. Nevertheless we leave together and I walk her back along the prom. We haven't gone far when she pulls me into a doorway and begins kissing me, her tongue straight into my mouth. I'm still recovering from the shock when she grabs my crotch. As a wave of revulsion comes over me, I push her away. No romance here.

The highlight of our week is the Adam Faith Extravaganza. Being a matinee, the audience's not big, but performances are, Emile Ford and the Checkmates being the first act.

'Wha' do ye wanna make those eyes at me for,
If they don't mean what they say'ye ……..'

They sound as good live as on the record I'd recently bought; a brilliant start to the show. A group of giggling, screaming girls are sitting on the row behind us. One of them leans over to Malcolm, loudly asking:' Is your cock hair the same colour?' The girls collapse into uncontrolled laughter. Malcolm has ginger hair; his face is even redder than usual.

Next on stage are The John Barry Seven; dazzling white suits and black shirts, John Barry himself playing trumpet as well as conducting the band with subtle flicks of his free hand. Lead guitarist is Vic Flick, amplified twangs of his Fender Stratocaster leading the instrumental numbers *'Hit & Miss'* and *'Walk Don't Run'*. Then Adam Faith strolls nonchalantly onto the stage, clicking fingers as he sings his latest hit.

'Someone else's bay-beh
Someone else's ey'ye's a'are blue'

He's quite short, dressed smartly in a light suit with slim-jim tie, blond hair tidily coiffured. Girls scream as he sings other hits; *'What do you want'*; *'Poor Me'*. However, his next song, *'Big Time'* is greeted not only by screams but also by shouts from a group of teddy boys on the balcony. Jealous of his fame and fortune, they walk out on the act shouting *'Big Dick'* in unison with Adam Faith's *'Big Time'*.

The rest of the week goes at a fast pace, though fractiously at times as arguments arise about what to do next. We buy a plastic ball and try to play soccer on the crowded beach. Sunbathers complain we're knocking down the kids' sand castles, so we stop. Rolling up our trousers, we paddle in the murky waves. 'Let's have a race on the donkeys' shouts Slim. Most of us decline, but Rocky takes up the challenge. Slim mounts the donkey facing backwards whilst Rocky, jockey-like, digs his heels into the poor creature's sides. The donkeys set off at a frightened and frightening pace. Within fifty yards, both riders fall off. No winner.

'Bugger off you punks' shouts the shocked donkey owner. 'Don't come here again.' We depart at speed.

Next stop, South Shore Pleasure Beach where I avoid the Big Dipper, preferring to go in the Fun House. The continually laughing model of an oversize clown outside this attraction doesn't amuse. To me it looks sinister; out of a horror film. Pub crawls on the last two nights of our holiday bring festivities, and financial resources, to an end and Friday sees us walking to the railway station rather than travelling by taxi. We pass Bloomfield Road Football Stadium, previously visited to watch Blackpool vs Burnley, as well as to see Stanley Matthews, wizard of the dribble. On the train I have feelings more of relief than exhilaration. Yes, it's been an exciting and

Don't Drink and Drive!

eventful week, but friendships have deteriorated, and I'm flat broke. I won't be doing it again in a hurry.

* * *

'I'm not going on that motorbike again!' Maureen, Len's fiancée, is adamant. They'd just been in an accident and, although nobody was hurt, it was enough for Maureen to refuse to ride pillion. In any case, she's certainly not the pillion passenger type; much too classy and sophisticated.

This is how I unexpectedly become proud shared owner of a motorbike. The *Ariel Leader* looks more like scooter than motorbike, encased in shiny blue and cream metal panels, hiding the 250cc engine. It also sounds like a scooter because of its two-stroke mechanism; more of a purr than a growl. A 'Mod' bike rather than a 'Rocker'. This is probably one of the reasons Mother, surprisingly, agrees to my taking over the machine. Little does she know that, in fact, it has quite a powerful engine with one of the fastest accelerations of any bike. Uncle Hubert's supportive, already owning an Ariel Arrow with the same type engine, which he takes every year to watch the Isle of Man TT. The theory is that faster acceleration makes the bike safer, the rider being able to pull out of difficult situations more quickly. I don't know how much water this theory holds, but it's enough to seal the deal, particularly with Hubert's support.

My *Ariel Leader* enables me to join the local bike gang, despite its 'Mod-like' appearance. All the others are on 'Rocker' bikes: *Triumph Bonneville*, *Matchless*, *Norton*, and the new *Ducati*. I'm able to match for speed, joining them on rides to *'Blubberhouses'*, a section of road between Skipton and Harrogate particularly suitable for high speed motorbike challenges. To do a 'ton' is the aim, though I don't have the confidence to match other gang members.

My relationship with the Ariel's not great. The machine often breaks down because of difficulty in mixing correct proportions of petrol and oil for the two-stroke engine. Spark plugs get oiled up and on a number of occasions I return pushing the bike rather than riding it, which Mother notes, raising doubts about my biking abilities. Rumours that I've joined a bike gang, joining them on high speed challenges over *Blubberhouses*, brings her to a decision. I'm no longer allowed to have the *Ariel Leader*. At first this comes as a major blow as I won't be able to join biker mates on adventurous rides to seaside towns, Blackpool and Morecambe. No longer will I impress the *'leather girls'*. But the situation changes remarkably, and in my favour!

Having lost the motorcycle, Len decides to buy a car. Although he's working as a 'tackler' at Broughtons Mill, keeping most of his wages, paying only 'board' to Mother, he doesn't have enough money to buy the car. Uncle Jim, as usual, has managed to find the perfect vehicle.

'It's a Rover 60, one careful owner; old lady who only goes out in it at weekends. Low mileage, well looked after by the garage' enthuses Jim.

His reputation as a wheeler-dealer has again come to the fore, though I have my doubts. 'Sounds too good to be true' I think, but don't say, not wanting to sabotage the deal.

Mother agrees to sell the motorbike and adds further cash to buy the Rover, on condition that I have a share in the car. Probably a bad decision, but who am I to complain? The deal goes through and the big, almost imperious, light grey Rover 60 arrives outside our house. Len polishes it with immense pride and it's greatly admired by neighbours, not accustomed to seeing such a vehicle on our council estate. Len quickly passes his driving test and begins giving me lessons, though not very successfully, since we argue too much. As it happens I already have a driving test arranged for the motorbike which I manage to change to a car test. There's not much time, so Len arranges a few lessons with a friend of his who has a driving school. He advises taking the test in the driving-school car, rather than the Rover, as it's much smaller and easier to manoeuvre.

Test day arrives, my confidence low. 'Don't think I've a hope in hell of passing the test' I think to myself. No doubt Len and the driving instructor think the same as we set off on the test drive.

'Turn left' instructs the examiner, which I do, remembering to activate the direction indicator; but unfortunately I fail to turn it off after completing the manoeuvre.

'It's because the car I normally drive has an automatic indicator turn off' I explain to the examiner who seems to accept this explanation, even though I make the mistake several times more.

'Turn right, stopping about halfway up the hill and put on your

Don't Drink and Drive!

handbrake whilst in neutral' instructs the examiner. 'Then perform a hill start.'

I manage the first part, but when trying to complete the manoeuvre, roll slightly back down the hill. Disaster! By now, having made several mistakes, I resign myself to failing the test. Unexpectedly, this relaxes me so I complete the remainder of the route more confidently, having nothing to lose.

'Mr Kershaw, you have passed the driving test, but must take more care with your hill starts. I almost failed you on that.'

I'm dumbstruck, managing only to mumble a quiet 'thank you'.

Len's also dumbstruck, as well as being somewhat disappointed since now he'll have to allow me more access to the car on my own.

* * *

Other than me, the main beneficiaries of a lucky driving test triumph are my mates, who seem to multiply as news gets round since I'm the only one with access to a car.

'Let's go to The Moorcock on Saturday' suggests Nick. 'There's a 21st Party there.'

I reluctantly agree and we meet at the Crown for a pint before setting off along the road towards Cowling and Keighley. There are six of us in the Rover, all laughing and joking; distracting me. It's also a terrible night weatherwise, blowing a gale, rain pounding on the windscreen. The country road's dark, Rover's headlights not the most powerful. I vaguely make out a sign, 'ROAD WORKS AHEAD' as an unlit fork in the road appears. 'Which fork to take?' I ponder; under pressure. Steering to the right proves to be a big mistake as the car bounces and shakes noisily over a partially completed new road. Barriers appear a few yards ahead, though I manage to slam on the brakes just in time. We all clamber out of the Rover to survey the scene. Across the barrier there's a drop of several feet, where soil's been dug out ready for hardcore and concrete. Shocked silence at our narrow escape as I manage to reverse out of the predicament and continue on our way, this time taking the left fork. At The Moorcock, the silence is broken almost immediately.

'We've been on the new by-pass even before it's been built' a gleeful Nick shouts to the whole pub. He trembles with mirth, though also in relief that the episode ended safely. The story does a round of the drinkers with other 'pals' describing the incident with great hilarity. I sit at a table in the corner in embarrassed silence.

A few weeks later it's another Saturday night. Arriving back late from taking Mother to visit relatives in Rochdale (another car access dependent duty), I've missed meeting up with my mates. I drive to *The Crown*. 'They've gone on to Nelson' reports the barman, 'said they were going to the Imp later to see Wee Willie Harris.' They're not in The Lord Nelson, our favourite pre-Imp pub, so I debate whether to join them at the dance hall since it's now after ten o'clock and entrance isn't cheap. I make what proves to be ae wrong decision. Parking outside the Imp, I go in, despite being short of funds. Not as many people as usual in the dance hall, so it doesn't take long to locate my drinking pals, four of them in the bar, together with four girls. 'You've missed Wee Willie Harris' shouts Slim. 'He was terrific. Went wild. Like a British version of Jerry Lee Lewis.' I buy a pint; first of the evening.

'Are you motorised?' asks Nick.

'Yes, but there's not room for all you lot' is my nervous reply.

'No problem. Rocky's walking Jane home. She lives at the boundary so there are only six of us.'

Doesn't seem a good deal to me, particularly since I'm the only one without a date; but I'm trapped. We clamber into the Rover, two boys and three girls squeezed into the back, Nick sitting in the front passenger seat. Everybody's quite fresh, except me, and I don't appreciate the hilarity and laughter, being sober and without a girl. 'Keep your hands to yourself' screams one of the girls, unconvincingly.

'Keep the noise down' I plead as we pass the police station. 'We're overloaded. Don't want to be stopped or there'll be trouble.'

Things quieten down, only the rustle of bri-nylon rara skirts and slurps of the odd necking session. I drive along Burnley Road towards Colne, making sure to keep within the speed limit as I've been stopped before in this area. Nothing much seems to be happening, though Nick continually glances at the back seat checking that his particular girl is not being accosted. As we near Albert Road, Colne's main street,

Don't Drink and Drive! 113

Nick suddenly bursts into life. Feeling he's 'missing out' stimulates one of his more hare-brained ideas to date.

'It's too early to go home and all the pubs are shut' he shouts to the otherwise engaged back seaters. 'Let's go onto the moors past Black Lane Ends. We can have a snogging session up there.'

This idea's greeted with enthusiasm by the boys; not as much by the girls; and not at all by me. But, as leader of the pack, Nick gets his way and I hesitate to acquire a reputation as a 'party pooper' as peer pressure holds sway.

I drive up the narrow, winding lane that is Skipton Old Road onto the moors, branching off at what's little more than a track. After a few hundred yards I park besides a couple of other cars in a lay-by regularly used by courting couples. It's totally dark and cold. Nick deserts me to join the back seat revellers, though by now there's not much revelling going on. Giggling and groping soon come to an end since there's little room for romance with six teenagers in the back of a second-hand saloon car. None of the girls are regular girlfriends of the boys. One begins to panic.

'I want to go home' Alison sobs, 'if Clive finds out I've been out on the moors with another boy, he'll dump me.' The other girls echo her sentiments.

'Yes. Let's get going' says Nick. Even he's disillusioned with the whole escapade so I start up the engine, reverse, and drive back to the road.

With relief, I head back towards Colne, a relief that makes me drive a little too fast. In the headlights, ahead seems to be a straight stretch of road, so I continue at the same speed, but nearing the bottom of the hill, I realize there's a bend. I slam on the brakes, but too late. A horizontally striped black and white post appears in the headlights, which I assume to be concrete. Closed eyes wipe out the vision. Everybody screams and yells, including the boys, as the Rover comes to an abrupt, shuddering halt. I've driven into the ditch at the side of the road. Everyone's silent; in shock, but luckily nobody's hurt, except for a few cuts and bruises. Nick and I get out of the vehicle to survey the damage. Nick's a motor mechanic at his father's garage, so knows something about cars. The black and white post lies flat on the ground behind the Rover – wood, not concrete.

'Doesn't look too bad' Nick assesses the damage. 'If we can reverse out of the ditch, we might be able to get it back on the road.'

Nick orders everybody out of the vehicle as I jump back into the driving seat. The engine starts first time and as I put the gears into reverse everyone helps push the car backwards, with success. Miracle of miracles! It's a sombre journey back to Colne.

'I can't tell mum and dad, or Clive, I've been in an accident on the moors at midnight' wails Alison. 'They'll murder me.' The other girls mumble their concurrence, as do two of the boys.

'You'll have to make something up, Roy.'

Thinking of my own parents' reaction, and particularly of Len's, I'm forced to agree. My mind races, in panic mode.

'What if I say we came back from Nelson along Barrowford Road? There are always accidents on that stretch of road.' I float the idea. 'I'll say there was a patch of wet leaves just before the bridge and that I skidded on them.'

Not much reaction from passengers, who are still in a state of shock, the girls sobbing quietly. Only Nick gives a nod of approval.

'OK. That's what I'll say. We'd all better stick to the same story.'

I drop people near their homes and park the Rover down the back street outside Len's house. Walking back home, I let myself in and go straight to bed. Mother and Father, fortunately, are asleep. Tossing and turning all night, I finally resolve to tell the truth. No good getting entangled in lies remembering Mother's quote from one of her respected authors, Sir Walter Scott:

'Oh what a tangled web we weave when first we practice to deceive'

Next morning I rise early and walk nervously over to Len's, who is already up surveying the damage.

'You've done it now' he says in an irritated rather than angry voice. 'You won't be able to use the car again. What happened?'

I tell him the full story, though understating the number of passengers and stressing I'd only had one pint.

'Don't know whether I'll get it on the insurance' Len adds, despondently. I return home, not telling my parents anything of what happened.

Later in the morning, Len walks up to the British Legion for his usual Sunday morning pint. He's greeted by Nick and Slim who tell him how

Don't Drink and Drive!

the Rover had skidded on wet leaves on Barrowford Road.

'That's a load of bunkum, and you know it' Len spills out.

Other drinkers gather round to hear the full story. Whoops of laughter greet sordid details, all except Clive, who seethes with anger when he hears Alison is one of the 'girls on the moors'. Another relationship bites the dust.

The Barrowford Road story's the one submitted to the insurance company.

CHAPTER 7

Education, Education, Education

'See Lowcock there in front of goal? Try and kick the ball to him; he might score.'

Mr Murphy, Lord Street County Junior School sports teacher, encourages me to centre the rain soaked, heavy leather ball. We're at football practice on the school playing field and I've been put on the right wing because of my speed. I spot Lowcock, who's shouting to me: 'Kershaw, pass the ball. Stop messing about.' Kicking the ball as hard as I can, it flies through the air landing just a foot in front of the centre forward, who manages to tap it over an imaginary goal line, between coats acting as goal posts. 'What a fluke!' I think.

I don't usually play football, but brother Len's given me a pair of his old Co-op Brand *Stanley Matthews* boots. They're too big for me; broken laces have been knotted together. Soiled blue and white hooped football socks are also too big, falling down round my ankles. Off-white baggy shorts stretch down below muddy knees. A claret and blue (Burnley colours) football shirt's torn and stained from years of Len's sweat. The image of a keen, smartly kitted, enthusiastic footballer I am not! A week later Mr Murphy draws me aside as I emerge from a classroom.

'Kershaw, I want you to play in the school team on Saturday, against Park School. You'll be outside right.' The request comes as a shock since Mother always says I'm the studious one, brother Len the sportsman. She probably won't approve of my mixing with 'rough' boys in a football match.

'No, I can't' is my whispered, less than truthful, reply. 'Mother's taking me to Grandma's on Saturday.' Mr Murphy looks disappointed and I feel crestfallen. But that's as it is.

It's not that Mother's against sport in general, only some types, particularly those that might interfere with academic progress. Swimming and athletics are okay, with long-distance running her main

Education, Education, Education

sporting interest, partly because Czech Emil Zatopek and Russian Vladimir Kuts are often seen winning long distance races on television. However, her hero's Gordon Pirie, a Yorkshire born runner who's challenging other international stars. We make a visit to White City in Manchester especially to see him; standing at the edge of the floodlit track, almost in touching distance as the lithe runner strides imperiously past, almost a lap ahead of struggling competitors. Another attraction of Pirie is his working-class background; unlike middle-class university educated British runners, Roger Bannister and Chris Chataway.

I'm youngest in the class at Lord Street Juniors. Accelerated progression through infant school, jumping two out of four classes, means I'm now ahead of my peer group. Mother's spent a lot of time teaching me to read and write. Birthday and Christmas presents are usually books, pens, coloured pencils. A small hand held blackboard, with accompanying chalk, is another present. Later, a chemistry set. Even comics are allowed, *Beano, Film Fun, Tiger, Rupert Bear Annual*, as a way of improving my reading grade. The aim? To ensure a place at Colne Grammar School and thence University.

'You better go to bed early tonight' instructs Mother. 'It's your 11-plus exam tomorrow.' I'm already feeling nervous. Unusually, Father intervenes.

'No, it's better for him to stay up a little longer so he'll be able to sleep. He can watch Arthur Askey in *Before Your Very Eyes*. It'll help him relax.'

Mother relents and I watch the hilarious show with its corny jokes and innuendo, Sabrina being the butt of many of Arthur's gags. The strategy works because I pass the 11-plus exam though only just ten years old.

Most working-class parents would have been happy with this outcome, but not Mother. She's discovered that one of my class mates, Eric Woodruff, is being allowed to go to grammar school a year early. Eric is son of the general manager of Colne Co-operative Society, of which my Father is President. Mother's peeved at this, seeing it as an insult to her adored son's intellectual prowess and Father's status in the community. She arranges a meeting with the Headmaster.

We wait in the corridor outside Mr Doig's office. Mother's trembling as she knocks on the door. 'Come in' orders a deep, authoritative voice.

We enter, Mother trembling even more, whilst I hide behind her in embarrassed silence. Mr Doig looks the epitome of a headmaster. Steely grey hair matches his steely grey eyes, which look piercingly at Mother. A lined, tanned face oozes charisma. Mother's not intimidated though; she dives straight in.

'Why hasn't my son Roy been put forward for early entry to the grammar school?' Her voice shakes with emotion. 'He's done better than Eric Woodruff in most of the school tests. And he passed his 11-plus early. Why are you holding him back?'

Mr Doig's taken aback by this aggressive approach, but manages to reply in a polite though firm tone. I shuffle even further into the corner of the office; face a deep shade of red.

'Mrs Kershaw, your son's doing well at school, but not as well as all that. Eric Woodruff's more mature and confident whilst Roy's too shy and reticent. I don't think he'd cope with the rigours of a grammar school education at this stage. In any case, Eric is almost a year older than your son.'

This doesn't satisfy Mother who continues to protest that I should be able to go to grammar school next term. Voices are raised; the headmaster begins to lose patience.

'Mrs Kershaw. I'm not going to discuss the matter any further. The decision's been made. Your son will go to grammar school next year, not this year. Please close the door as you leave.'

Mother strides out of the office, dragging me behind her. In a final act of defiance, she doesn't close the door.

'Pompous old git' she mutters under her breath. 'Trying to keep the working class down.'

* * *

The following year, Mother opens the letter from Colne Grammar School. It's a list of clothing and equipment I'll need for school, which starts in just two weeks time.

'How are we supposed to afford all this lot' questions Mother. 'They must assume we're made of money. You'd think he's going to Eton!'

Blue School Blazer – available from Odhams Gentlemen's Tailors.

Education, Education, Education

Dark Grey Worsted Trousers – from the same source.
School Tie – blue and grey stripes.
White Shirt.
School Cap – must be worn when coming to or leaving school.
Oxford Shoes – black
Leather satchel
Full rugby kit in school colours
Cricket 'Whites'
Shorts and plimsolls for PT
Cross Country running pumps

'It's a good job Len's working now or we wouldn't be able to afford all this. Don't know how Mrs Thornton's going to manage for her Brian. Mr Thornton's out of work.'

A warm, sunny Monday morning in September greets the first day at my new school. I look smart in my uniform, walking down Townley Street with a spring in my step. A crowd of children jostle at the bus stop, but only two are wearing the blue school uniform. Most of them are from the council estate and, having failed their 11-plus, are attending the local secondary modern. 'Grammar Grub, Grammar Grub' shout boys who I previously counted as pals. I feel downhearted. Two buses arrive; one for the grammar school, one for the secondary modern.

Alighting from the bus I join other pupils walking through impressive wrought iron gates, along a pebble covered driveway. Crunch of pebbles and sound of eager chattering fill the air. The school's modern, but built in Georgian Style. Pale brown sandstone sparkles in the sun, as do multi-paned rectangular windows. The main entrance has imposing columns at each side of large oak doors, but we're directed to a side door. Entering the main hall we're guided to the two front rows of what seem a myriad of collapsible chairs; boys left, girls right. Two rows of teachers are already seated on a large stage, most in gowns, some even wearing mortar boards. Chattering stops when the Headmaster, Mr Phillips, swishes onto the platform. He's a tall, well-built man with thinning black hair brushed straight back exposing an enormous forehead. Striding to the lectern, he turns to face eager young faces gazing up at him in awe. No 'welcome' to his new charges; just a brusque introduction to the first hymn.

'We'll begin this morning with hymn number 35 - *We Plough the Fields and Scatter.*'

The Headmaster's booming voice announces start of a no-nonsense school year. A music teacher plays an introduction to the hymn on an old upright piano and the whole school bursts into slightly out of tune song.

As it happens our first class is with Mr Phillips: 'Speech Training'. He writes on the chalk board

'*The Lord Mayor was a terrible scornful man ....*'

'Kershaw, please read that out loud.' I stand up and nervously begin reading, almost in a whisper. 'Speak up. We can't hear you' shouts the Headmaster.

'T'lord maya wer a terebel scooornful man ......'

'That's the worst I've ever heard anyone speak' scolds an exasperated Mr Phillips, glaring at me across the classroom. Other classmates titter. 'You'd better practice at home. You won't get anywhere with an accent like that.'

I do practice at home, but under my breath and in the bedroom where parents can't hear. Mr Phillips perseveres for another few weeks, but finally gives me up as a 'lost cause'. I'm the only one in class not to pass the end of term oral test, but it doesn't worry me. All my family and mates speak exactly as I do.

* * *

My grammar school career's largely successful. Academically I'm usually in the top three in end of term exams. In sports I'm selected for rugby, basketball and swimming school teams; even for cricket, despite only taking two wickets and scoring eight runs throughout the season. I become junior athletics champion, though partly as a result of changed rules. A new sports master, Mr Lancaster, decides that classification into juniors or seniors should be based on age rather than which form a pupil's in. As youngest in class, I'm designated a junior for annual sports day and since many of my class move up to seniors, they no longer compete in the same events. I win most junior races, as well as shot-put and 'throwing the cricket ball'. Mother attends sports day, swelling with pride as I'm presented with the cup.

I'm channelled towards science rather than arts subjects for GCE 'O levels', partly because they're my best subjects, but also because it's Government Policy to emphasise science and engineering. Government has decided that the economic future of Britain lies in research and investment in technology based industries. Both Mother and I recognise this, and also that future jobs are likely to be in these sectors. Lack of an aptitude for practical subjects is ignored, and a yen for politics, history and music put on a back burner.

GCE results are good, though not outstanding. I manage to scrape through French; surprised I even pass. Our French teacher's local, speaking with a strong Lancashire accent with which she manages to endow the language and little French is actually spoken in lessons. As it happens, a trade union leader from Paris, Monsieur Fabius, a colleague of my Father, is staying with us. I'm studying in my bedroom, swatting for the following day's French oral exam when Monsieur Fabius knocks on the door and comes in.

'Bonjour, Roy. Je habite près de la Tour Eiffel.' I'm non-plussed, not understanding what he's saying.

'Sorry. What did you say?'

Monsieur Fabius repeats in French and then in English.

'I live near the Eiffel Tower.'

Doesn't augur well for tomorrow's exam!

Another surprise is that I get my best mark in English Literature. The reason for this is partly down to an exceptional English teacher, Mr Land, but also because of books set for the exam: *The History of Mr Polly* by H G Wells catches my imagination from the first line.

'Hole!' .... *'Ole'* .... *'Oh! Beastly Silly Wheeze of a Hole!'*

Portia's speech in Shakespeare's *Merchant of Venice* also grabs my attention:

'The quality of mercy is not strain'd
It droppeth as the gentle rain from heaven .... '

Despite an increasing interest in the Arts, my success in science subjects and continued pressure from teachers to concentrate on a technological career, persuades me to take maths, physics and chemistry in the Sixth Form.

* * *

I continue to do well in end of term tests, but other distractions begin to undermine progress. Appointed captain of the school football team, I also join an amateur team, Brierfield Crusaders, who play in a local league. Going to Turf Moor to watch Burnley, who are doing well in the First Division, is another priority. In Summer I play in a Sunday cricket league for a youth club, as well as watching Lancashire League cricket at Colne's Horsfield Ground. Sport's all consuming, taking up a lot of my time. However, the main distraction from studies is my continued relationship with working-class friends. Many have started work and are therefore relatively flush. We go out most Friday and Saturday nights; sometimes mid-week. Drinking and smoking at pubs and coffee bars; seeing the latest films at the many local cinemas; playing snooker in dodgy snooker halls and the British Legion; chasing girls at dance halls, particularly the Imp. We're immersed in pop music, listening to the radio at every opportunity, watching *Top of the Pops* and *Six Five Special* on TV.

All this costs money, so, though I get a little spending money from my parents, I have to find other ways of raising funds. A Sunday morning paper round falls into my lap. Though arduous (I have to carry two heavy bags of newspapers over a long, long route), it's lucrative. An early start's also a problem, particularly when suffering from a hangover after a late Saturday night. A small commission from a weekly collection round for the Weavers Union, arranged by my Father, is another source of income. In school holidays I manage to get a number of jobs; labourer with an uncle's building firm; operator of a cloth measuring and folding machine at one mill; 'loom oiler' at another.

My first morning in Bannisters weaving shed's a shock. A wall of tremendous noise almost bursts delicate, unaccustomed ear drums. The atmosphere's thick with cotton dust creating a haze through which feeble early morning light filters from large dirt covered windows.

Education, Education, Education

I'm wearing an oversized, oil stained one-piece overall and an old pair of boots. The ancient foreman has a friendly but knowing smile as he hands me the long, tapered metal oilcan with which I'm to keep weaving industry wheels turning. We go round the back of the first loom.

'Ye've gorra pur oil int' them three bearin's' shouts the foreman, lips an inch from my reverberating ear drum. He points through the clanging, whirling wheels and cogs of the scary mechanical monster. 'Ollos tek a't fluff w'it tip of t'can before ye pur oil in……… an' dunna catch t'oilcan in't spokes.'

'Training Course' over, I commence my duties as sole oiler in the eighty loom weaving shed. Things go better than expected as I slip into an extremely boring, but effective, rhythm. No distractions since the noise obviates any chance of talking with weavers or tacklers. Only one hic-up when I catch the nozzle of the oilcan in a flywheel. The metal casing's shredded and dragged out of my startled hand as oil spurts everywhere and the loom comes to an abrupt, grinding stop. The weaver glares at me through a tirade of curse-laced invective. I can't hear what she says, but nothing's left to the imagination. 'Stupid young bugger' are the only words I can decipher from reading her taught, mobile lips.

At break time I go to the canteen where I'm invited to sit at a table by a kindly weaver. Two young apprentices are not so kindly.

'A' thee from t' BBC?' shouts one of them. 'Ye talks like ye are.'

This comes as a surprise to me since, at school, I'm still considered to speak with a broad Lancashire accent. 'Must be losing my working-class roots' I worry.

'Ye won't get far wi' those lilywhite hands in this business' shouts another. 'Bet ye've neva done a days hard graft in yer life.'

I look down at my pristine, artistic fingers in dismay. A tackler joins in the taunting:

'Ye betta work a bit slower. Ye'll make it difficult fer Fred when 'e gets back to work. 'E can't keep up wi' a young 'en like you.' Others murmur in agreement.

Nearing the end of my four weeks as loom oiler, the foreman invites me to his office. I'm not popular with the other workers and expect to be reprimanded in some way, but to my surprise I'm complimented.

'Roy, ye've done reet well int' job. Usually we 'ave at least one loom fire a week, but while you've been workin' we 'aven't 'ad any!' The foreman, who I now know as Ted, continues in all seriousness.' A can give ye t' job wi' increased pay, if ye want it.'

I'm quite appreciative of the kind words and reply in what I hope is not too dismissive a tone.

'Thanks for the offer, Ted, but I have a place at Manchester University starting in September so I'll be leaving Colne.'

Ted sighs but still gives me a warm smile. We shake hands and I leave with warm feelings of friendship for a man who has helped my initiation into industrial life.

A more ignominious way of raising cash is by misuse of weekly 'dinner money'. Home is some distance away from the school and there's no one there during the day, both parents working. Therefore I have my dinner at school, which has to be paid for. This particular week I'm desperately short of funds so keep the 'dinner money'. Before school each morning I put food items in my satchel from home; bread, cheese, meat leftovers and perhaps a hardboiled egg - enough to tide me over until our evening meal. I continue this deceit for several weeks. Mother notices I'm eating more at supper.

'Glad to see your appetite's improving. Good for the brain.'

* * *

A crowd of fellow pupils surround the school notice board. Pushing to the front, I search for my name on a recently pinned up list. Barkley, Dewhurst, Fairbrother, Jones ……….. Murphy. No Kershaw! My stomach sinks. I haven't been chosen to join the ranks of temporary GPO postal workers. My luck's out and it's going to be an impecunious Christmas. Walking dispiritedly along the corridor I feel a tug on my blazer sleeve. It's Alan Peters, a posh classmate. 'OK for him' I think to myself, 'his dad's got plenty of money, so he won't go short.' His father used to be a cotton mill owner, but the building's been converted to an intensive broiler chicken shed.

'Curly, why don't you come chicken catching at my dad's new broiler business? It's well paid and you'd only have to work a few hours for three days. Early in the morning, so no need to miss school.'

It's a tempting proposition so a few days later sees me cycling down

Education, Education, Education

to the Waterside former weaving shed. It's four in the morning, cold, damp and dark. My hands are frozen, which doesn't help in the ten minute 'training course' provided for new recruits. 'Ye've te carry four chickens in each 'and, one leg between each of yer fingers' mumbles the foreman. 'Charge 'and 'll put chickens in yer 'ands. All you've te do is carry 'em t't loadin' bay.'

Sounds impossible to me, but that's the job I've let myself in for. We're led into a huge dark shed. Surprisingly little sound from hundreds of chickens crammed together in battery cages, just a rustle of feathers and the odd squawk. The smell's horrific, like being trapped in an ammonia filled vat. Inches of litter and droppings squelch under our feet on the concrete floor.

'Lights a' pur on every two 'ours' explains the foreman. 'Then t' conveyors start movin' an't chickens gobble down't pellets, peckin' each other in't process. They fight to get a't pellets.'

Fluorescent tubes light up, immediately followed by a burst of clucking and cackling as unfortunate chickens scramble over each other to get at the pellets and mash poultry feed. Creaking conveyor belts move slowly, squealing as they traverse rusty wheels and cogs. The lights go out, but there isn't complete darkness since a few lit bulbs enable us to vaguely see our prey. A chargehand thrusts an inverted chicken into my hand, quickly followed by another three, but I drop one of them.

'Ye'd better tek' three in each 'and to start we' 'til ye' get used to it' says the impatient 'chicken catcher'. 'Ye'll 'ave te increase te four in quick time though.'

A few days later everyone's gathered in the school hall. It's the last day of term and we're eagerly awaiting permission to leave early to start the Christmas and New Year break. The school's divided into houses, Boulsworth, Noyna and Pendle, with me the elected 'House Captain' of Noyna. The time at which a particular House is allowed to leave depends on points gained or lost during the term. Boulsworth pupils are first to leave, at lunch time, followed by Pendle shortly after. 'Noynarites' remain in their seats, frustrated and peeved. The Deputy Head's seated at the front of the hall, at a desk on which lie record books for each House. I ask to look at the Noyna book. Shock! Horror! One of the reasons Noyna are last House to be released is that points have been deducted: 'Kershaw. Late twice and absent on a third day without sufficient reason'. I manage to keep an inscrutable expression on my face whilst shuffling guiltily back to my chair.

* * *

Despite extra-curricula social and romantic distractions, I continue to progress well with my studies. I apply to University of Manchester Institute of Science and Technology (UMIST) for a place in the Chemical Engineering Faculty, though not because of any great enthusiasm for engineering. Indeed, my lack of practical know-how is a family joke. Part ownership of a motorbike and a car has not resulted in acquisition of mechanical skills. 'Double-declutching' or adjustment of 'ignition timing' is not part of my vocabulary. I don't know how to change an electric plug or washer in a dripping tap. Even gardening's beyond both my competence and interest. No; the reason I've chosen chemical engineering is that I won't have to focus on any one specific scientific subject. The degree course will provide a more general engineering qualification.

The University has set three A-levels at B Grade as condition of entry to the honours degree course. Teachers consider this well within my capabilities and I sit the exams with confidence. Chemistry and physics go well; no problem in reaching the required grades here. But maths is a different matter. A question on 'relativity', a topic I've struggled with all term, stumps me. I get bogged down, continually having to retrace my steps through the calculations. As a result, I fail to finish the maths paper, achieving only a C Grade, thus failing my attempted university entrance. A few days after results are announced, I sit disconsolately in the school cloakroom, trying to raise my spirits by singing:

'Life is just a bowl of cherries
Don't take it serious, life's too mysterious .....'

A school friend comes and sits next to me. 'You don't sound convinced of that' he comments sympathetically. I decide to seek advice from Miss Jackson, our maths teacher; highly respected in the school. Her teaching skills are not the reason for my failure.

'Roy, I'm disappointed you didn't manage to reach the required grade. The problem is that, because there aren't a lot of facts and written material to learn in maths, students don't give enough time to it.' I nod in agreement. 'You have to concentrate on worked examples. As I remember you didn't complete all the maths problems and tests set for homework?' Again I have to shamefacedly nod in agreement.

'Don't get disheartened though. You're quite capable of achieving a B grade, even an A, if you work hard enough. I'll do all I can to help if you decide to retake the exam next year.'

Miss Jackson's words encourage me to stay on in the 6th Form and my family, particularly Mother, are fully supportive, despite extra financial pressures. The following year I achieve required grades in all subjects and am accepted on the degree course at Manchester University. A sigh of relief all round.

* * *

In my first year I don't get involved much with university life, returning back to Colne at weekends; the call of romantic liaisons too strong for the attractions of, what is said to be, an exciting Manchester night life. Mid-week visits to the College Club, a gambling and striptease venue frequented by students, often end in drunkenness and empty pockets. I join the Labour Club and go on demonstrations in support of Che Guevara; black beret and red star badge de rigueur. Otherwise my focus is on a blossoming relationship with Janet. Music wise, Bob Dylan's *'The Times They Are A'Changin'* is the student anthem.

The chemical engineering course itself is, on the whole, boring and practical aspects continue to be my 'Achilles Heel'. I fail Technical Drawing and don't perform well in laboratory experiments. A technical language course in either German or Russian has to be taken, and in a fit of bravado and political aspiration I choose the latter. The exam paper's in Cyrillic Script of which I don't have a clue; even unsure as to which way up the exam paper is! Optional courses on management and work study, as well as computer programming, are more interesting, providing some credits.

My university career's almost brought to an end when Janet's pregnancy results in an early marriage. Thoughts of quitting university are considered, but parents' offer of free accommodation and Janet continuing to work in fact makes us better off financially. I travel each day to Manchester by train, allowing time to study on the journeys and we go out to social events only occasionally. An unexpected result of my changed, ostensibly more difficult, circumstances is that I'm able to focus on my studies. Final exams are faced with confidence and I manage to obtain a Class II Division I Honours Degree in Chemical Engineering. 'If you'd done better in your practical exam and handed in your dissertation on time you'd probably have gained a First' advises a friendly professor.

Mother and Janet attend the award ceremony, both in smart new suits; Mother also has a new hat with matching handbag and shoes; hair is expensively permed. A contented, triumphant smile lights up Mother's face. I look at her joyful demeanour, thinking 'Yes, you've every right to that smile. My success is largely due to you.'

But I don't say it.

* * *

Part of the degree course, at the end of the second year, is attachment with an industrial engineering firm. Amongst those listed is Mullards, an engineering firm based in Burnley. Though Mullards is an electronics rather than chemical engineering enterprise, its proximity to Colne persuades me to apply for an attachment there. The assignment's to be in the company's research department. I send in a completed application form, but have a shock when I'm not accepted. One of the questions on the form is 'Do you have any links with the Communist Party?' Of course I answer 'Yes' to this given that my parents, as well as many of my wider family, are committed and well-known members of the Party. Security Service rules don't allow my involvement in what could be politically sensitive industrial research.

Instead, I'm found a placement at Hardman & Holden, a sulphuric acid manufacturer in Clayton, a run-down industrial area of Manchester. It's a grey, damp Monday morning as I travel by bus through the desolate landscape. The Plant's surrounded by a high stone wall, stained almost black by fumes and smoke from decades of toxic emissions. A gateman at the main entrance directs me to Reception, a

Education, Education, Education

small, new, brick building, dwarfed by the corrugated iron roofed factory structures nearby. Here I meet up with two fellow undergraduates, also from UMIST.

'We'd better get you into some proper work clothes' says the foreman allocated the task of looking after university 'greenhorns'. We change into oil-stained, greasy brown overalls, with oversized white laboratory coats, also stained. Yellow safety helmets are too large and don't fasten. Our 'office' is a small, broken-down wooden shed at the edge of the industrial complex with one desk and chair; a wooden bench; table with gas ring to boil water in a battered kettle; and three metal mugs. Our assignment's to prepare a 'heat and mass balance' over the whole plant in order to identify opportunities for saving on energy costs. Everyone knows there's little chance of anything useful coming from the exercise in the few weeks available, but at least we'll be kept busy.

Next morning we enter the 'hell' that is the sulphur conversion plant. Bright yellow sulphur's being shovelled into a bubbling cauldron of the molten chemical by muscular, bare-chested labourers. The heat's horrific, as is a pungent smell of sulphur dioxide, despite noisy efforts of a crude ventilation system; a living version of a 'fire and brimstone' horror story. The noise from diesel engines spraying molten sulphur into the furnaces is deafening, regularly brought to a crescendo as blasts of air burst into the combustion chamber. Blue flames can be seen through small, opaque furnace windows. We move into the main plant as quickly as possible.

Here, what seem miles of large metal pipes, some black, some silver, snake angrily round the vast space, reaching up to an elevated, vaulted ceiling. High pressure jets of steam regularly burst from pipes and cylindrical metal vessels that contain the gases and liquids needed to produce sulphuric acid. A network of steel stairs follow pipes round the plant, regularly interrupted by platforms accommodating a myriad of valves, meters and measurement devices. Noisy 'heat exchangers' are everywhere, as well as large, clanging pumps to keep liquids and gases on the move. To fulfil our assignment we'll have to climb up this honeycomb of metal stairs to read gauges, turn valves on and off; and search for leaks in the system, of which there are many. I don't relish the prospect. The next two weeks are spent crawling and climbing all over the wretched, dirty and noisy machines and equipment.

From time to time sirens blare, but nobody seems to take any notice. My ungloved hands are frequently burnt on unlagged hot water pipes and it's easy to slip on the greasy metal steps. I have visions of falling from a great height into a vat of molten sulphur or, even worse, sulphuric acid, finishing up like a victim of the 'acid bath' murderer, John Haigh. Nightmares follow as I imagine the whole plant exploding in a ball of fire because I've left a valve open, releasing a stream of sulphur dioxide and scolding steam.

I resolve never to become a chemical engineer!

Returning to University I visit the careers office to search for alternative job opportunities. Most of the positions are for engineering graduates, so I make an appointment with the Careers Officer, Mr Spencer, who I've previously spoken to. He's aware of my aversion to chemical engineering.

'Roy, have you thought of becoming a teacher?' queries the friendly careers advisor. 'It's a very rewarding job and much better paid than students appreciate.'

He shows me the pay scales for newly qualified teachers, as well as for department heads and headmasters. Better than I expected.

'In the past you've mentioned the possibility of spending a year as a VSO. Does that still apply?' I explain that, now I'm married, that wouldn't be possible.

'Have a look at this, then' continues Mr Spencer.

He shows me a leaflet with a photograph of a young British graduate, dressed in white short sleeved shirt and baggy khaki shorts, surrounded by a group of black students.

'As part of the British Aid Programme for Uganda, graduates are offered a year at a teachers training college in Kampala, followed by two years teaching in a local secondary school. Would you be interested in that?'

My spirits rise. I'm more than interested, rushing back to Colne to tell Janet the good news.

'No, no, no' she screams. 'I'm not going to leave England and my family to live in a mosquito infested jungle in Africa!'

Impossible to reason with her in this mood, so I return to the careers office for further inspiration.

Education, Education, Education

This time I look more carefully through the piles of leaflets and prospectuses, spotting a glossy brochure with '*Co-operative Wholesale Society*' printed prominently on the front. '*Management Training Scheme*' the leaflet continues. 'Could this be the opportunity I've been looking for?' I ponder. Contacting the CWS Chief Recruitment Manager, a Mr Hardacre, I manage to get an interview. He's impressed with my enthusiasm and commitment to co-operatives, putting me forward for the formal selection process which I come through with flying colours. Mr Spencer rings me up.

'Heard you've managed to get a job on the CWS Management Training Scheme. Well done! Your perseverance has paid off. Best of luck in the future.'

I thank him for his kind, encouraging words. I'm in a mood of exhilaration as I ponder my success since the Post has a high salary and includes a year at university to study management. Based in Manchester, only twenty five miles from our home town, Janet will also be pleased she doesn't have to go to Uganda! But most of all I'm excited to be working for a socialist, working-class organisation, much to the acclaim of both Mother, Father and my wider family.

In the words of the song – '*Who could ask for anything more?*'

Good News! A letter arrives from the CWS:

'Dear Mr Kershaw

We are delighted to offer you employment as **Management Trainee** *with the Co-operative Wholesale Society. The Terms and Conditions are set out in the attached contract of employment.*

You should report to Mr Sherwood, Head of Recruitment, at New Century House in Manchester on Monday, 15th October at 10.00 am.

Please review this offer of employment, sign the note of acceptance, and return to myself.

Yours faithfully

Mr John Steeple - Head of Human Resources

It's my dream job! Well paid, based in Manchester, not far from Colne. The appointment includes a year at Salford University, studying for a Diploma in Advanced Studies in Management. Mother will be over the moon that I'm working for the Co-op. In the afternoon I walk down by the river to meet Janet on her way home from work. Waving the letter in the air, I run to greet her with the fantastic news.

'Janet, I've got the job' I shout above the sound of rushing water in the nearby river. My joy's unbounded and Janet's face lights up as she takes in the message as we walk hand in hand along the river bank.

'Does that mean we'll have to move to Manchester?' Janet asks warily. It would be her first time away from home.

'Yes. We'll have to rent a bed-sit until we can find a house' I reply.

'Suppose we'll be mixing with your university friends. I might feel out of place.' Janet considers the downside of the new appointment.

'I've met the people I'll be working with. They're a great bunch. We'll have a good time, and plenty of money. With our savings, we'll be able to put down a deposit on a house in no time.'

A smile comes back to Janet's face as we continue to walk home in joyous mood. The sun shines more brightly; birds sing more sweetly.

CHAPTER 8

Politics, Politics, Politics

Two police cars are parked on the recently tarmacked street near Janet's family home. Several police officers can be seen searching an area of waste land that at one time had been an allotment, but is now used to dump domestic and other rubbish. The whole area's cordoned off with yellow and black police tape, forbidding entry; warning inquisitive locals not to venture into what is a crime scene. More policemen are on the waste land, struggling to put up a large yellow plastic tent. It's a cold, frosty Saturday morning in late December and Janet and I are visiting her parents before the New Year. We stop to ask a constable what all the fuss is about. 'Can't tell you anything' he responds, so we continue the short walk to the familiar end terraced house.

'What's happening?' I ask Janet's dad as we enter the kitchen through the back door. 'There's loads of police out there.' Both parents look strained, Edith almost in tears.

'There's been a murder on the spare ground behind Talbot Street' Granville informs us in a quiet, muffled tone. 'Rumour is that it's the girl who lives in the house across from our back yard. The end house.' It's a distressing situation; my in-laws are very upset. We'd occasionally seen the teenager, a quiet, mousy-haired girl, but had never spoken; not even knowing her name. She'd always kept her head down, eyes focused on the pavement, coat collar pulled up allowing only a glance at her pale face. We commiserate with Janet's parents and Sister Irene.

Over the next week, more information filters through. The murder victim was indeed the girl from the end house across the back. Sixteen year old Joan Robinson had gone to her first dance down the Imp where she'd been picked up by a young man, escorted back to Colne on the last bus, then dragged onto spare land near her home before being sexually assaulted and strangled. Rumours circulate that the murderer had forced pieces of wood into her vagina; a particularly vicious attack. The murder has cast a deep depression over the town, matched by a rainy, cloudy morning with blustery wind as cotton workers return to local textile mills after the Christmas/New Year break. On the buses, instead of the usual gossip amongst mainly female textile workers – weavers, leesers, office staff – updating all and sundry about exciting events over the holiday period, there's a dispirited silence.

It didn't take long for police to apprehend the culprit, but it came as a shock, particularly to Janet. Brian Marsden was arrested at his parent's house on North Valley Road, near the bottom of Townley Street and my own family home. Both Janet and I knew him by sight, but Janet had a closer link as she'd worked with Marsden's mother in the leesing department at Bannister's Mill. Though they hadn't been friends, Janet nevertheless felt some sort of bond with a former work colleague. Difficult for us both to comprehend how the son of a quiet, hard-working mother could have carried out such an evil deed.

* * *

The silent face speaks of evil; depravity. Cold, yet vacant eyes seem to penetrate my psyche and a hard, surprisingly pretty face reflects incomprehensible turpitude. Lips curl in a contemptuous expression; almost a smile. Myra Hindley's image, full front-page of the *Daily Mirror*, stops me in my tracks. Inside pages have a smaller picture of Ian Brady and a report on the trial of the most detested couple in the country. I go into a cafe to read the full report, trying to understand how such things can happen.

The Moors Murderers, Ian Brady and Myra Hindley, are on trial for the killing of 12 year old John Kilbride, 17 year old Edward Evans and Lesley Anne Downey, aged just 10. Edward Evans had been viciously murdered with an axe at Brady's home in Gorton; John Kilbride abducted from a market in Ashton-under-Lyne; and Lesley Anne Downey snatched from a fairground on Boxing Day in 1964. Both children had been sexually assaulted, their bodies buried on Saddleworth Moor in shallow graves. The news report gives details of a tape played to the Court which had been found in a suitcase at Manchester Central Railway Station left luggage, along with nine pornographic photographs taken of a young girl, naked, with scarf tied across her mouth. The tape records Lesley screaming and pleading for help with Hindley heard threatening to hit Lesley Ann if she didn't shut up.

'I must tell you summat, please take your hands off me a minute, please .... Please Mummy, please .... It hurts me, I want to see Mummy, honest to God ...... please God, help me .... leave me please, help me, will you .... I've got to go because I'm going out with my mamma.'

My blood runs cold. Saddleworth Moor's only 25 miles from Colne, near Manchester where I'm at University. I'd even visited the pub near the University campus where Brady had tried to pick up other homosexuals. I'm also campaigning for Sidney Silverman, Labour MP for Nelson and Colne, who's guiding a Bill through the House of Commons to abolish capital punishment. Many people in Colne, now including me, are questioning whether the death penalty should be banned when such horrendous murders have been committed just a few miles away.

* * *

Wages of Sin Ought To Be Death

Joe Sunter, *Colne Times* feature writer, puts forward his view on the death penalty:

'The wages of sin is, and ought to be, death. If some vile and perverted scoundrel subjects a young and innocent girl, say, to horrors and terrors too infamous to be detailed except under oath, and of necessity in a court of law, ought to be destroyed by an outraged society'

The headline and article strike deep. I've been corresponding with the local newspaper for some weeks now over the abolition of capital punishment. This headline will require yet another 'Letter to the Editor'. The *Colne Times* has been attacking Sidney Silverman for months on the death penalty issue. After 20 years of campaigning, Mr Silverman had managed to introduce a private Member's Bill suspending the death penalty, resulting in 'The Murder (Abolition of Death Penalty) Act' in 1965 which had been passed in a free vote in the House of Commons by 200 votes to 98, and in the House of Lords by 200 votes to 104. However, this Bill doesn't reflect the views of the *Colne Times* editor – or the majority of Colne residents and voters. I spend much of my time arguing with friends and family, even Mother, about this controversial issue. In letters to the newspaper I complain about the quite scurrilous campaign against Mr Silverman, not only on his stand as an abolitionist, but also on account of his opposition to the Vietnam War and support for nuclear disarmament. There's little support for my view that the death penalty should be abolished, either in other letters to the newspaper or in personal debates.

'An eye for an eye and a tooth for a tooth is what I say' challenges my brother-in-law.
'An eye for an eye leaves the whole world blind.' I quote Gandhi.
'In any case' I continue 'we don't follow this principle in our justice system. If someone attacks another person causing, say, grievous bodily harm, we don't allow the victim to attack the perpetrator in revenge, do we? Just because hanging's convenient doesn't make it right.'
Mr Silverman writes to the *Colne Times* with statistics from around the world which indicate that the death penalty is unlikely to deter people from committing murder. The Editor responds, saying that even if a few people are deterred, this will at least save some innocent lives. Our MP writes back pointing out that there have also been miscarriages of justice when accused people have been hanged, despite later evidence showing them to be innocent.

The debate goes on – and on, and on.

* * *

The Government calls a General Election in 1966, to be held on 31st

Politics, Politics, Politics

March. Although Labour had won the previous election in 1964, a majority of only 4 MPs has made it almost impossible to govern, so Harold Wilson has decided to go to the Country again. I join the campaign in support of Sidney Silverman.

I'm a nervous and reluctant canvasser. The idea of knocking on a stranger's door and asking them to vote for a Labour candidate fills me with trepidation. What if the householder's a Conservative? Will I get a mouthful of abuse? Even more likely; what if the person answering the door is not political and I've interrupted his or her viewing of Coronation Street or Double Your Money? Maybe I'll lose the MP more votes than I gain! But these imagined responses are nothing compared with the vilification I receive in this particular election.

We're canvassing in a working-class area of known Labour supporters where steep cobbled streets have rows of stone terraced houses down each side. It's a dismal evening, the pavement wet from earlier rain as I knock on the door of the first house, opened by a short, middle-aged man with an expanded beer gut. He's wearing a worn, striped shirt with sleeves rolled up past the elbows exposing muscular, tattooed forearms. Baggy trousers are held up by braces, though the size of his girth makes them somewhat redundant.

'I'm canvassing for Sydney Silverman your Labour candidate in the General Election' I manage to blurt out. 'Can we count on your vote?' His face contorts with rage, turning an unhealthy red, a thought passing through my mind that he may be having a heart attack.

'No, you bloody well can't' he shouts. 'I'll ne'er vote Labour again. He shouldn'a be protecting murderers and perverts.'

I'm stunned into silence, only managing to mumble a few words about Silverman's record in helping the people of Colne. It takes all my courage to move on to the next house. This time a textile worker answers the door still in working clothes from her occupation as a weaver. I repeat my opening gambit.

'Silverman's protecting murderers. String 'em up, is what I say.' She yells. 'An eye for an eye and a tooth for a tooth is what the Bible says.' I try to respond.

'But the Bible says 'Thou Shalt Not Kill' doesn't it?' She closes the door in my face.

The next elector's more reasonable. Again she's a weaver.

'I've always voted for Mr Silverman, but this time I won't vote at all.' She has gentle eyes and explains that, after the Moors Murders, she can't bring herself to vote for the abolition of capital punishment. We need to protect our children is the sentiment.

I continue down the street as lights begin to appear through curtained sash windows and street lamps flicker into orange glows as dusk descends. Hurrying past a house with a 'Vote Conservative' poster in the window, I come to the last house on the row, bigger than neighbouring properties, with a view of the river valley. The door looks to have recently been painted red. There's a small stained glass window over the door, light from inside the house shining through blue, red and yellow pieces of coloured glazing. I lift the ornate knocker and give two raps. This time a smartly dressed woman, with glasses and neat hairstyle, answers.

'Good evening' I greet her with my politest voice, judging her to be a teacher or solicitor.

'Do you expect to vote for Sidney Silverman in the forthcoming election' I courteously ask.

'Certainly' she replies in a refined Lancashire accent. 'Silverman's been greatly misrepresented in the press. He's a courageous man with high principles.'

I move on with a slight spring in my step, but canvassing reverts to the previous negative response levels, so I decide to report back to the committee room. Other canvassers have had similar experiences so I resign myself to the probability that Silverman, who's been our MP since 1935, will lose the election this time, mainly because of his prominence in the 'stop hanging' campaign.

The election's even more fraught with danger for Silverman because there's an additional candidate; an Independent by the name of Patrick Downey. Although Mr Downey's a Labour supporter from Manchester, he's also the uncle of Lesley Anne Downey, one of the victims of the Moors Murderers. He's standing solely on the ticket of retaining capital punishment, with strong backing from both national and local press.

Election Day arrives. I go round with Len Dole, the Labour Agent, to 'knock-up' known Labour voters who haven't yet appeared on returns from 'tellers' at the polling stations. Len's surprisingly optimistic.

Politics, Politics, Politics

'Roy, don't look so glum. Sidney's been MP for nearly thirty years. He's done a lot for the area so voters won't desert him, particularly in Nelson.'

I remain despondent, however, and don't go into the Count, waiting outside the Town Hall along with a crowd of other supporters. Labour officials go in looking tired and somewhat downhearted, having worked hard all day at the various committee rooms. News begins to filter out of the Town Hall. 'There's been a good turnout, particularly in Nelson'; 'Patrick Downey's getting a lot of votes'; 'Silverman seems to be ahead'; 'The Tories are looking glum'. A few smiles begin to flicker on the faces of Labour supporters outside, including my own. When the result's announced a few hours later there are whoops of delight both inside and outside the Town Hall. Sidney Silverman has won with his biggest ever majority!

Analysing voting figures the next day, it's clear what has happened. Although Silverman's vote has gone down since the 1964 General Election (from 20,205 to 18,406) the Conservative vote has declined even further (from 17,561 to 13,829). Most of Patrick Downey's 5,117 votes have come from erstwhile Conservative voters.

* * *

The headline in *The Guardian* reads:

'Massacre in My Lai'

It's accompanied by a graphic photograph of maybe twenty bodies of partially clad peasants, mainly women and children, strewn on a farm trail near a Vietnam village. The newspaper report describes how more than 500 unarmed civilians had been brutally killed in an unprovoked attack by US troops. Seventy killed and thrown in a ditch; a child gunned down whilst running away. Another villager, hands raised begging for mercy, murdered by a soldier.

As an active Labour Party member, I join with others in calling on the Wilson Government to resist pressure from Lyndon Johnson to send British troops to Vietnam. Successfully. More horrific news filters through; napalm used to destroy plants and vegetation, and to burn the skin off subsistence farmers and their families, inflicting incredible pain. Thousands of bombs have been dropped indiscriminately in both North and South Vietnam and there are continual reports of US atrocities against defenceless people. 'We must do something to stop this' I challenge myself. An opportunity arises later in the year when a protest demonstration at the American Embassy in Grosvenor Square is organized. I catch a train to London, joining the March on its way from Trafalgar Square. The scene's chaotic as thousands of mainly young protestors crush along the wide streets, waving banners and placards, shouting slogans.

'Hands off Vietnam'; 'Stop the Bombing'; 'Make Love, not War'; 'Hey, Hey LBJ, how many kids have you killed today'? Some sing anti-war songs.........'How many deaths will it take till he knows, that too many people have died? The answer is blowin' in the wind'.

Others shout abuse at the many police officers, some with truncheons flailing, trying to control the crowds. Police on horseback move in, forcing marchers into the road from pavements. Horses whinny and plunge into the melee. As we near the Embassy, police try to form a cordon, preventing protesters from entering gardens in front of the imposing, heavily protected building. But they can't stop the swelling throng of marchers which moves like a giant swarm of wasps. Policemen fall and suffer injury. Protestors fall and suffer injury. Many are arrested, thrown into police vans that have forced their way through the crowds. The noise is deafening; shouting, whistling, screaming. Some have drums, beating an insistent rhythm as background to the surrounding mayhem.

After a couple of hours I force my way through the demonstrators, heading back to the railway station since I've a train to catch. Running down the platform I just about manage to board before the train pulls out. Carriages are crowded, not with demonstrators but with suited businessmen returning to their suburban homes after a day 'bean counting' in the city. Pushing my way into the bar I find myself standing next to a couple of slightly inebriated stockbroker types who are confronting a young female student dressed in denim jeans and jacket, still carrying a placard; 'Stop the War'.

'You should be at home studying, not attacking and injuring our police' bellows one of the 'suits', his companion nodding vigorously

Politics, Politics, Politics

in agreement. The student stammers, unable to withstand this barrage of criticism. I butt in, angrily asking:

'Why are you getting so worked up about a few cracked shins and bruised ribs?' I demand to know, voice trembling with emotion. 'Even at this moment there are probably hundreds of poor, innocent Vietnamese being bombed and shot; villages and farms destroyed.'

The businessmen fall silent for a few seconds before blustering and ridiculing my heart felt tirade. I walk away, flustered, but content I've had my say; optimistically hoping my arguments may have at least dinted their supercilious, uninformed opinions.

* * *

The group of Japanese Buddhist Monks float silently into the Church Hall. Saffron robes sway, jet black hair glistens. They carry maybe eight, six foot high vertical, oriental style banners depicting photographs and hand-printed images of a devastated Hiroshima after the first H-bomb, 'Little Boy'; dropped by an American B-29 bomber, the *Enola Gay*. The Buddhists are touring the UK with their graphic exhibition and have been invited to our CND group in Manchester. Pictures and images have been toned down, pastel shades surrounding softened black and white photographs, seem to make them even more horrific, leaving the full impact to imagination. The Mushroom Cloud of a nuclear explosion. Black, charred corpses of men, women and children spread-eagled in the streets with only outlines remaining of some bodies incinerated in the blast. White skulls are piled high. Destroyed buildings, still in flames, stretch into the distance; total devastation. Other photographs are of people dying from radiation sickness, months after the blast, bodies covered in erupting spots and scabs, bleeding from ears, nose and mouth.

A legend is printed on one of the banners:

80,000 PEOPLE KILLED, 90% OF THE CITY DESTROYED

Everyone remains silent. No questions.

* * *

Janet and I board the coach booked to take CND supporters down to the latest march in London. Banners and placards are stored overhead.

NUCLEAR ARMS; NO – PEACE; YES

NO MORE HIROSHIMAS

Protestors are wearing large badges, made by one of our group. All bear slogans: 'Students Against the Bomb'; 'Teachers Against the Bomb'; 'Miners Against the Bomb'; 'Rockers Against the Bomb'. Janet and I are there as 'Extremely Nice People Against the Bomb!'

Arriving in London we join the march from Trafalgar Square to Hyde Park. There are thousands of people, but the march is much quieter and better organised than the Vietnam protest. No crushing or conflict with police who are, on the whole, friendly and helpful. Some shouting of slogans, but in joyous and positive spirit. Much humour and laughter with a jazz band adding rhythm and excitement to the demonstration. Symbols of Peace abound. Picasso's gentle White Dove of Peace; Rainbow Striped Flag of Peace, purple, blue, azure, green, yellow, orange and red with 'PACE' printed on many of them. Most striking of all, is the distinctive black and white CND Symbol; simple but impressive.

Incongruously, the sound of Martial Music suddenly fills the air. 'Land of Hope and Glory'; 'Rule Britannia'. As we pass, a large banner drapes from an upper window of Conservative Party Offices.

Communist   **N**eutralist   **D**efeatist

By the time we reach Hyde Park, we're at the back of the demonstration, having dawdled to admire historic sights. I'm dismayed to find that, instead of a homogeneous crowd of like-minded people, there seem to be innumerable splinter groups, each with their own hastily constructed stall. Communist Party of Great Britain competes with the Marxist/Leninist Party. Trotskyites, Maoists, Workers Revolutionary Party, Democratic Socialists, Socialist Workers Party all display pamphlets and leaflets espousing their particular, often narrow view on how to reach a socialist ideal. On a platform in the middle of the Park, Michael Foot's making a speech, arms waving, silver-grey hair sweeping down over his forehead. It's difficult to hear what he's saying, despite a microphone and public address system having been installed. Anarchists crowd round the front of the stage, waving their peculiar triangular flags, some black, some with the anarchist symbol, a capital A surrounded by a capital O. They're hissing and mumming threateningly, the sound drowning out many of Michael Foot's inspirational words.

We travel back home somewhat dispirited.

* * *

'Naught For Your Comfort'. A book appears on Mother's 'bookshelf', in fact the windowsill, which is used as temporary storage for the latest tracts. It's a hardback book, deep blue dustcover including a head and shoulders picture of a grey-haired Priest, hands raised in eloquent pose. I've seen the image before in the Daily Worker. Father Trevor Huddleston's book is riveting, detailing the wrongs and social injustice caused by the Apartheid System in South Africa. I read it with ever increasing anger, a sense of shame that white South Africans could impose such degradation on the majority black population. But I don't take the matter any further, being more absorbed with Vietnam and CND campaigns.

A headline in *The Guardian* brings Apartheid back into my focus:

'Dozens Killed in Sharpeville Massacre'

A photograph of men, women and children, mainly children, lying dead, scattered on a dusty track, accompanies the journalist's report. 'More than 50 black people killed when 300 police officers open fire randomly into a 6,000-strong crowd outside the municipal offices in Sharpeville, protesting against the apartheid pass laws and other humiliations. Scores of injured have been taken to a Johannesburg hospital with gun-shot wounds' continues the report.

A Boycott Movement has started in UK putting pressure on the South African Government to rescind obnoxious apartheid laws. Our local co-operative joins the boycott, removing Outspan Oranges, Grapes, tinned South African Fruit, and other foods from the shelves. Our family supports this action, but, with a pang of guilt, I don't join the Anti-Apartheid Movement (AAM). Too much on my plate already.

BBC news brings seemingly endless reports of droughts, famines and wars in Africa and Asia. The television screen's full of images of starving mothers and children, bloated stomachs, vacant eyes without hope. Crops wither in the fields, skeletal animals collapse from exhaustion as wells run dry. Background music brings tears to my eyes; Barber's *Adagio*; Elgar's *Nimrod*; incongruously, Tchaikovsky's *Romeo and Juliet*. I vow to become a VSO after graduation.

* * *

There's a sharp rap at the curtained window. Sat comfortably in the living room of 17 Temple Street, on a weekend visit from my home in Manchester, we're watching television, The *Benny Hill Show*, *The Good Old Days*. Another rap at the window. Drawing back the thick curtain a face appears, glowing in the reflected light of a blazing coal fire; a handsome, weather worn face, greying hair still sporting a roguish curl in the centre of his forehead. Uncle Frank, Mother's brother, has arrived. I shuffle to the front door in my carpet slippers and open it, shivering slightly as the cold evening air pushes in.

'Come in, Frank. It's cold out there,' but he declines.

'No. You're only watching that rubbish on TV. Ought to be ashamed of yourself, all that education and a university degree, wasting your time and intelligence. TV's taken over from religion as 'the Opiate of the Masses'.' Frank wastes no time in quoting Karl Marx. 'Come out with me. I know a terrific pub near Hebden Bridge where there's folk music, poetry, and people actually talking!'

I'm reluctant to leave the warm, cosy fireside, but slight feelings of guilt force me to acquiesce. 'Some truth in what Frank says' I reflect. Putting on a thick woolly jumper and brown duffle coat, I follow him down the steps, heading towards his pride and joy; a Bond 'Mark C' three-wheeler car cum motor cycle. It's old and decrepit, black paint scraped and muddy, small plastic windows scratched and opaque through wear and tear. Frank isn't interested in image, only that the vehicle gets him from A to B at minimal cost. He's never passed his

Politics, Politics, Politics

driving test, but is still able to drive the 'Mark C' because it doesn't have a reverse gear, so a motorbike licence is enough.
'You'll have to give me a push. Starter motor's not working' Frank intimates.
I do as he bids and in a few yards the 200cc engine splutters into life. Jumping into the passenger seat of the two-seater machine, we accelerate to 30mph, effective top speed of the clapped out engine. Frank struggles with the large steering wheel as he leans forward to wipe condensation off the inside of the windscreen with an oily rag. The whole frame of the three-wheeler rattles as we trundle along country lanes over the Pennine Moors. Headlights aren't very bright and the way Frank's straining to peer at the road ahead makes me doubt his eyesight's as good as he makes out. 'Twenty, Twenty Vision' he maintains, despite evidence to the contrary.

It's a good hour's drive to reach *The Hare and Hounds* in Hebden Bridge. Frank applies the breaks as we enter the car park, allowing time for them to become effective. It's a relief when we come to a halt just before imminent collision with a stone wall. The pub's a blaze of light through many wooden framed windows as we walk towards the main entrance. It's also a blaze of sound; heated, but friendly, conversations; folk songs sung with strong Yorkshire accents; 'Another four pints of *Sam Smiths*, Fred' shouts a regular to the smiling, rotund landlord. Entering the public bar we're greeted by a chorus of welcoming calls. 'Ey there Frank. A' ye' givin' us a song teneet?' A murmur of approval sweeps round the room. Frank's a trained tenor and likes nothing better than to sing famous arias to an appreciative audience. *Your tiny hand is frozen* from La Boheme; *Figaro* from The Barber of Seville; *Nessun dorma* from *Turandot*; and my own favourite, Handel's *Where'er you walk*. Frank doesn't disappoint his fan club, vocalizing *Celeste Aida* with great feeling, his voice warm, rich and gentle – a lyric tenor.

We eventually sit down in a corner of the room near a roaring wood-burning fire. The atmosphere's thick with smoke and smell of tobacco. Polished brasses adorn distempered walls, interspersed with paintings of Yorkshire scenes: A gushing waterfall at Hardcastle Crags; colourful barge on Rochdale Canal – blue, red and green traditional patterns of roses and castles with copper nameplate *The Pennine Way*; winter scene at Crimworth Dean, dry stone walls and rocky outcrops emerging from the deep snow. All painted by local artists. Raised voices in dialects I can't understand and laughter at smutty jokes that I can understand. No women in the room, so language is uninhibited.

'Your Mum tells me you've been on demonstrations in London against the Vietnam War and nuclear weapons.' Frank begins to talk politics. 'About time you rebelled against America and the capitalist system.' I don't react, knowing it would likely lead to an argument. 'Are you going to join the Communist Party?'

'No, I'm not. Quite happy in the Labour Party, thank you' I reply. 'At least the free market system allows people to demonstrate and speak openly. Don't see that happening in Russia; or China for that matter.' I have a little dig. Frank shakes his head and sighs, unable to respond.

'Glad to see yer workin' for't Co-op though. I expect 'Divi' to go up this year' Frank jokes. 'Co-ops 'er working-class organisations. There are lots of them in Russia, all owned by the People.'

I try not to respond to the statement, which is meant to draw me into the socialist fold, but can't resist.

'Yes, I'm glad to live in a country that allows people to form co-operatives of their own free will. In Russia, they're established by the State with people forced to join. They don't work. Look at the collective farms; they can't even feed their own people.' Frank reacts angrily.

'Communism's streaking ahead. First into space, most gold medals in the Olympics, industrialisation dragging Russia and Eastern Europe into the 20th Century. There's no stopping the march forward.'

'It won't work if people aren't free. I work for the co-operative movement, a system I agree with and support. But other people want to go into business on their own, which in Britain they can. If you want to work for Government, you can. If you want to work for a multi-national, you can. Even if you want to opt out of society altogether and form a commune, you can; and get paid benefits at the same time! In Russia you'd have no option except absorption into a monstrous government bureaucracy.'

Frank's stunned into silence. It's unlike me to speak so forcefully and I immediately regret undermining his sincerely held principles in such a graphic way. I feel guilty; a traitor to long held family values.

An embarrassed silence is broken by one of the local artists making

Politics, Politics, Politics

his way over to our table.

'Frank, the pencil and charcoal drawing I've been doing for a couple of months is finished. Hope you like it.'

He lays the framed picture on the table. It's of Frank's head and shoulders, lined face straining forward with an expression of both determination and compassion. 'There must be something better than this' it seems to say. Frank can't let the politics drop.

'It's communism that's freed the working class, put them into power. We'd still be slaves without the efforts of radicals and revolutionaries.'

I try to keep my cool; but can't.

'Frank, you're blind to what's happening in Russia. People are being forced along one path. They're not free and if they disagree with Government, it's the Gulag for them. Surely you must see this by now?' I continue. 'If you try to force feed someone, they'll spit it out. This is the fatal flaw of communism however idealistic it may appear. The result is a more and more oppressive regime as people refuse to comply with increasingly onerous dictates.'

We leave the *Hare and Hounds* dispirited but, surprisingly, Frank shows no anger.

CHAPTER 9

Transition

I'm to take up my position with the CWS in just two weeks' time, so Janet and I travel to Manchester looking for suitable short-term accommodation. Cheetham Hill's our first port of call since there are many flats available at relatively low rents. We soon discover why. Cheetham Hill's a rundown part of Manchester, the high tenement buildings looking on the point of collapse. Graffiti on walls are partly covered by washing hanging out of upstairs windows. Many shops are boarded up with paint peeling off. Pre-Victorian stone walls are black with years of smog, belched out from industrial revolution chimneys. Like Coketown in Dickens' *Hard Times*. Incessant Manchester drizzle adds to the gloom as we continue up the road trying to find flats for rent, as advertised in the Manchester Evening News. It's a maze of dark alleyways, overflowing rubbish bins and broken down doors, many without numbers. We're turning to make our way out of the desolate area when an old black Austin car stops at the kerbside. Out jumps a huge bulk of a man wearing a threadbare black suit and trilby hat, his long bushy black beard glistening with sweat and drops of rain.

'You looking for accommodation?' he shouts in a strange mix of Jewish and Lancashire accents. We nod. 'I've got just the place for you. Jump in the car and I'll take you there, you'll love it. Just the place for a smart young couple.'

We clamber into the dirty back seat of the Austin and are driven just a couple of hundred yards further up Cheetham Hill Road.

'Here we are' says the enthusiastic prospective landlord as he opens the creaking car door, 'it's on the first floor.'

We climb the narrow, uncarpeted flight of stairs, footsteps echoing in the undecorated entrance hall. The landlord flings open the door, almost breaking it off its hinges. Peering into the dark, so called two-roomed flat, we're dismayed, though the landlord continues his

Transition

optimistic sales pitch. A double-bed takes up most of the space in the room, with only a chest of drawers and two wooden chairs squeezed into a corner. A small curtained alcove is termed a 'wardrobe'. Description as a two-roomed flat is partially correct since a tiny kitchen can be seen through a doorway (no door) on the other side which is reached, presumably, by climbing over the bed. We can't get out fast enough. There's a look of genuine shock on the face of a bemused landlord.

We catch a bus to Chorlton-cum-Hardy where I'd been in digs during my first year at Manchester University. Chorlton's not the most salubrious Manchester suburb, but certainly better than Cheetham Hill. We alight from the bus to be greeted by a huge advertising hoarding:

Emigrate to Australia for only £10
Children go free!

The poster includes a picture of a family on the beach in glorious sunshine under a clear blue sky. Small children are shown playing happily in the sand, all with big smiles. From the perspective of a cold damp Manchester, this sounds hugely attractive. 'No wonder people flock to this imagined antipodean paradise' I sigh.

We walk down the main street passing a butcher, baker and several other small shops, reminiscent of a village. There's also a Co-op self-service store; a big plus. Entering the busy post office I ask directions to a street where a newspaper advert promises: 'Luxurious bed-sit for rent – all modcons'. It's only a few streets away so we look round the property, which is on the first floor of a private house. Hardly luxurious, but good enough to put down a deposit.

The following week I borrow what's now exclusively Len's Rover. He's reluctant, given my previous track record, but as we've a lot of things to take with us, he relents.

'You'd better be more careful this time. No speeding. The brakes aren't as good as they should be, so don't take any risks.'

Driving cautiously, we arrive in Chorlton without incident.

'Look, Janet. That's where I was in digs' I explain, whilst leaning over to point down a side street.

I take my eyes off the road for a few seconds as the car moves over the brow of a slight incline. Too late! A Ford Anglia has stopped at a zebra crossing to let pedestrians cross. Jamming on spongy brakes only partially curtails momentum. There's the crunch of bending metal and squeal of tyres on a damp road, as well as a smell of burning rubber. It all seems to be happening in slow motion.

Janet screams: 'All our savings will be gone!'

The Ford is pushed onto the zebra crossing, but fortunately pedestrians have managed to avoid the encroaching vehicle. I get out of the Rover, as does the Ford driver, a neatly dressed youngish woman with coiffured auburn hair. She seems quite calm as we move to the pavement. A helmeted police constable appears on the scene and, after checking that there are no injuries, begins to question the lady driver as to what has happened. The constable speaks into one ear of the young woman.

'You should report him for dangerous driving, or at least driving without due care and attention' he urges. I speak into her other ear.

'Please don't do that, it was an accident. We're here to start a new life in Chorlton. My wife's distraught' I plead.

The wonderful Chorltonian refuses to press charges. Both Janet and I sigh with relief.

Though badly damaged, both cars are still in working order. After exchanging details we drive away from the scene, the Rover with police escort. We park the car outside our new bed-sit building, returning to Colne by bus. Len isn't angry, but sympathetic, probably having a conscience about the faulty brakes. The Rover proves to be a write-off, but again Len manages to get something on the insurance (he knows the local insurance agent well). We also learn the reason for the other driver not pressing charges; she's the wife of the local insurance agent who doesn't want to get mixed up with a court case which would be bad for business. My charmed life as a driver continues.

Things don't go well in our 'luxurious bed-sit for rent - all modcons'. Although our landlady, Mrs Penny, is kindly and sympathetic, she suffers from 'nerves', taking sleeping pills and an assortment of anti-depressants. Notices in entrance hall and stairs beseech; 'Please don't make any noise late at night or early morning'. The room itself is quite large, well furnished, and comfortable. A sofa converts easily, though noisily, into a bed. The minimally carpeted wooden floor is threadbare in parts, resulting in an echo as we traverse the room. There's even a small black and white TV. The main problem's the kitchenette which is quite small, partitioned off in one corner of the main room. It's also adjacent to Mrs Penny's bedroom, a thin party-wall providing little sound insulation. Kitchen surfaces are metal, including sink and draining board, stove and fridge with plenty of crockery, pans and cutlery to make a noise with, which we do. Janet has a reputation for clumsiness, *'Dainty Dinah'* from *'The Beano'* being one of my pet names for her. I'm not much better.

Mrs Penny looks quite drawn, her lined face pale and sad, with straight black hair tightly drawn back, stretching her skin over sharp cheek bones. She confronts us as we return from work one evening.

'Janet, must you make so much noise in the mornings? I'm only just managing to get to sleep when the crash and clatter of pots and pans wakes me up. You've the TV on too loud. Sounds like you're holding a dance when you bounce across the floor in the evening. *Please* be quieter, my nerves can't take it.'

Mrs Penny brings rubber mats for use in the kitchen. We keep the volume down on the TV and take our shoes off, creeping silently across the room. But to no avail as Mrs Penny continues to slide into a depressed state; so we start looking round for alternative accommodation.

However, a few days later sees a remarkable transformation in Mrs Penny's demeanour. Answering a knock on our door one evening reveals a changed woman. A smile transforms normally stern features and bright eyes express relief.

'Roy, I've good news for all of us. Friends of mine, Mr & Mrs Barnes, have rooms to let at their house in Stretford. They're a bit hard of hearing, so the noise you make won't be as much of a problem.' I take slight offence at the comment, though this is quickly overridden by a suppressed whoop of joy.

Next day, Saturday, we catch a bus to Stretford where Mr & Mrs Barnes, a lovely old couple in their seventies, greet us with warm smiles, offering a welcoming cup of tea and freshly baked buns. It immediately feels like a home from home as we follow Mr Barnes up narrow stairs.

'Mrs Barnes can't climb the stairs these days, she has a bad heart' intimates Mr Barnes. 'You can have all of the upstairs.'

This includes a large living room; separate dining kitchen, two double bedrooms and a bathroom. The contented smile on Janet's face reflects my own sentiments. And that's not all. The house is only twenty minutes walk from Old Trafford County Cricket Ground where the swashbuckling West Indian all-rounder, Clive Lloyd, is captain of a successful Lancashire team with England fast bowler Brian Statham backing him up with unerring accuracy. Even better is the proximity of the other Old Trafford where the 'holy trinity' of Charlton, Law and Best are leading Manchester United to unbelievable heights of footballing perfection.

* * *

My 'dream job' is not all I'd anticipated. Though the management training scheme's well thought out, the problem is my relationship with other trainees. Most of them are confident extroverts, putting my own diffident, introverted personality in the shade. I find it difficult to speak, resulting in tongue-tied reticence. Nervous exhaustion begins to affect my appetite and instead of looking forward to next day at work, I begin to dread daily competition with often arrogant, largely middle-class 'go-getter' types. My strong accent doesn't help even though we're in Manchester, home of Lancashire dialect. My only trainee friend, a working-class college graduate from Witan, recognises my predicament and offers advice.

'Don't be intimidated by these windbags; you're better than they are. Just imagine them with their trousers down, sat on the toilet; everybody's the same then! That's what I do, anyway.' His homespun philosophy and down to earth humour are a big help.

Once the induction period's over, things get better as we're sent to different departments in New Century House, to learn about the vast organisation that is the headquarters of the Co-operative Movement. My first assignment is in Market Research; all statistics, graphs, newspaper cuttings and customer surveys. Ventures into city shopping centres to undertake in-person questionnaire surveys are not successful. I'm too shy to stop people in the street. Telephone surveys are even more problematic as I freeze, unable to pick up the phone again after a number of rejections.

Transition

The Accounts Department's more congenial. A vast room with rows and rows of high, sloping wooden desks; dark brown lids, tall stools to match. Wood panelled walls are also brown, with only faint illumination from high windows. The gloom is lifted a little by a series of dispersed brass, banker's table lamps. Huge ledgers lie open on the desks; almost Dickensian. All that's missing are quill pens, ceramic ink pots and flickering candles. There's even a tall, wiry clerk with red hair, wearing a crumpled black suit; my mind's image of Uriah Heep in David Copperfield. 'Can this be for real?' I ask myself. I knock and enter the Chief Clerk's office who's in discussion with a smartly dressed young man who has ballpoint pen and clipboard in hand. The discussion seems quite heated.

'Mr Smithson, you'll just have to accept that your department's going to be integrated into the CWS computer system. The decision's already been made by the Chief Accountant, so you better get used to the idea. There's no way back.' The consultant leaves in a huff.

Mr Smithson welcomes me into the office with a warm handshake. Despite the recent altercation, he still has a smile on his face. His balding head, fringed by grey, neatly parted hair, is reddish, as is his chubby, yet wrinkled face. A tweedy, check suit includes a waistcoat, gold pocket watch chain dangling. Defiant eyes observe me over precariously balanced pince-nez.

'These young, inexperienced, so-called consultants think they know everything. They aren't the ones who have to work overtime and at weekends to sort out problems with computerised accounting. It's me and my staff.'

Clearly the Chief Clerk will have to be dragged kicking and screaming into the computer age. I doubt it will happen.

My next attachment's in the Computer Division. The main office is bright and airy, fluorescent lighting casting an artificial glow over a relatively small number of metal desks. Down one wall are punch card machines, preparing data to input through adjacent teletype equipment into mainframe computers. I count only six smartly dressed young office workers, mainly girls, operating the state of the art equipment. Two typists sit at their desks with large audio earphones fighting with bouffant hair styles. Mr Rebel, shirt-sleeved office manager, is busy scanning through computer printouts. I introduce myself.

'Can't deal with you just now. Jane, give Mr Kershaw a cup of coffee, will you?'

I sit on a patent leather visitors chair in the corner of the room, sipping the hot drink and flicking through an array of computer magazines scattered on a small coffee table.

'OK Mr Kershaw, let's go through the main office. I'll explain what we're up to.' An impatient Mr Rebel describes procedures and equipment at breathtaking speed. 'We'll go into the Main Frame Computer Room.'

The big glass door can only be opened through a coded pad. We walk in quietly; almost like entering a holy shrine, a room so spotlessly clean and air conditioned it could be in a hospital operating theatre. Two banks of grey metal cabinets, over six feet high and stretching the length of the room, house the Main Frame. Large spools of film-like tape can be seen through glass windows in the cabinets. They wiz round at great speed, but are almost soundless.

'By next year we'll have all CWS accounts controlled by this main frame computer' Mr Rebel enthusiastically exclaims. 'It will give us a chance to compete in the modern business world.' An image of Mr Smithson comes floating back.

Next, I'm seconded to the Work Study Department which involves an assignment in London at the CWS offices in Leman Street. Floor after floor of typists, clerks, office boys, girl Fridays, salesmen, bookkeepers and assorted administration staff. Everyone rushes round answering phones, entering ledgers, typing at breakneck speed. It's like living in an enormous abandoned bee-hive that's been taken over by swarms of ants. Mostly worker ants.

Part of the Management Training Scheme is an academic year at either Manchester Business School for an MBA (Master of Business Administration) or Salford University for an AdvDMS (Diploma in Advanced Studies in Management). The MBA's the most prestigious qualification and I'm interviewed by a senior lecturer from the Business School.

'Mr Kershaw, why did you join the CWS management training scheme, and how do you think an MBA will help your career?'

I answer nervously, stressing commitment to the co-operative movement and my desire to reach a high level management position in the CWS. The interviewer seems impressed with my responses to his questions, but there's a sting in the tail.

'You're clearly an imaginative and determined young man with a lot to offer. But you haven't looked me in the eye at any time during the interview, which usually means a person's untrustworthy, or very shy. With you it's certainly the latter. Do you think you'd be able to live with the intensely ambitious business graduates who attend our MBA Course?'

Put so bluntly, I have to accept this is unlikely. I take a place at Salford University; much more my scene.

* * *

Janet's disillusioned with her job prospects. She manages to find employment at a textile mill, in the spinning department, but is shocked at the rough and ready antics of big city mill girls.

'What the f... were you doing eying up my boyfriend on Saturday night?' curses Moira, in an Irish twang. 'I'll rip your f...... eyes out if you do it again.'

Mavis, the target of the cursing, turns round and grabs Moira's hair.

'Like to see you bloody well try' she reacts. 'He fancies me more than you.'

A brief fight ensues until the mill whistle announces start of work.

Cursing and swearing are the order of the day. Fighting's not unusual, particularly if anyone dares to criticise 'Georgie Best' the Manchester United footballer. The charge-hand's constantly mocked and ridiculed. Janet tries to stick up for the unfortunate woman, but is swiftly put in her place. We scour the *Manchester Evening News* for other jobs.

TRAINEE GPO TELEPHONIST

At least School Leaving Certificate required

Must have pleasant speaking voice

Female applicants preferred

Please apply to the Chief Engineer, Manchester Central Exchange

Janet's nervous about applying for what is regarded as a quite prestigious job. Would her broad accent be a drawback? Are qualifications good enough? In the event doubts prove unfounded as she sails through the tests and interviews, proudly taking up her position as GPO telephonist in one of the largest exchanges in the country.

We now both have well paid jobs, mine particularly so. Having saved for the deposit on a house, largely through Janet's wages and the generosity of her parents in providing free accommodation, we're now in a position to buy our own home. A suitable house is soon found, an almost new semi-detached bungalow on a middle-ish class estate. It's out of Manchester in Boothstown, overlooking the East Lancs Road to Liverpool. A regular bus service into town enables Janet to reach the telephone exchange each morning. We get on well with our new neighbours, another young childless couple; husband an aero-engineer working on Hawker Siddeley's Nimrod. Uncle Harold sells us his car, which he no longer uses after the death of his daughter, Clarice. It's a dark green Morris Minor, low mileage and reliable. We take our first holiday abroad, flying to Cala Millor in Majorca by Boeing 707, meeting up with a young unmarried couple there, and having a great time. We hire cycles to explore the verdant countryside; olive and almond groves abound, as do vineyards. We sunbathe on warm sandy beaches, though both of us get sunburnt. Back in Boothstown I get involved with the local Labour Party, becoming secretary of the Trades and Labour Council, much to Mother's delight. I'm also voted onto the Members Council of Manchester and Salford Co-operative Society. Sunday mornings I clean the Morris, parked on our newly asphalted drive and, looking along the tree-lined avenue, many neighbours are doing the same. We have our own home, a car, plenty of money, and careers with good prospects.

I should feel wonderfully happy; but I don't. Dreams of 'Changing the World' are fading fast.

* * *

Changes are made to the management training scheme, which had been meant to last another two years. The scheme's judged ineffective

Transition

since trainees are missing out on real responsibility. No experience of management at the sharp end. A 'sink or swim policy' is adopted with trainees placed directly into line management positions. With my chemical engineering degree, I'm moved to a production unit, the Edible Oils and Fats Factory in Irlam on the outskirts of Manchester. Familiar Co-op Brand Silver Seal and Gold Seal Margarine, as well as Avondale butter, are made here. I'm to be one of two shift production managers reporting to the factory manager. Shift work, 6 - 2 and 2 - 10, is not to my liking, but the job itself's fine. Six foremen report to me from butter blending, margarine production, and other departments. Head foreman, Harry, fortunately takes me under his wing and his protective influence is enhanced when it comes to light his wife works with Janet at Manchester telephone exchange.

By far the biggest costs of margarine production are the vegetable and fish oils used in various blends. I design a system to closely monitor and control use of the oils, saving significant amounts of money for the factory bringing me kudos and respect, despite my lack of experience and management skills.

An onsite research and quality control laboratory closely checks hygiene standards in the factory, an important aspect of food processing. The laboratory also develops new margarine blends; with some success. A Product Development Panel meets regularly to taste new blends and I'm on the Panel along with other highly qualified technical staff, including two PhD's and several graduates, as well as shop floor representatives.

'Is this what all my educational achievements and hard work are for; to assess marginal differences in taste of a mass produced fat spread?!' I ask myself. 'Surely I can do more than that?'

Such qualms, along with a lack of ambition to climb a competitive managerial ladder, makes me fundamentally question whether I'm on the right path. I resolve to change career and follow an inner compulsion to work in developing countries.

Janet's reaction is explosive. Normally placid, when reaching a certain level of frustration, all control's lost.

'I don't want to go to Africa' she screams. 'We've a home, good jobs and family. Why do you want to throw it all away?'

No point in trying to discuss the subject when she's in this frame of mind so I let the matter drop, though a few weeks later contact the

Overseas Development Administration (ODA) and go down to London for discussions. By now Janet's calmed down and is not so adamantly against an overseas adventure, particularly since I suggest it would only be for a couple of years. Talks with the ODA are not fruitful however, since opportunities to work as a VSO aren't practical, particularly as Janet's now expecting our first child.

'There are no opportunities in Africa these days explains a sympathetic ODA Officer. 'Most African countries are independent now and want to get rid of the British, not take on more. Colonialism's a dirty word these days.'

I return home disappointed and disillusioned. We continue our lifestyle and at least we have the birth of our baby to look forward to.

I always read the Guardian Appointment Section, usually focusing on opportunities for 'ambitious young graduates', though I'm not particularly ambitious and it's now some time since I graduated. On this occasion, however, another job advertisement catches my eye. It's for a 'Co-operatives Officer, BSIP'. The word 'Co-operative' always jumps out at me, so I look more closely at the advert, particularly as it's been inserted by the ODA. 'What does 'BSIP' mean?' I ask myself. Is it some sort of qualification, like a BSc or even OBE? Reading further, BSIP turns out to be an acronym for 'British Solomon Islands Protectorate'. The appointment is for a Co-operatives Adviser in the Pacific Island territory; still under British administration.

* * *

A few months later Janet and I are on the platform at Manchester's Piccadilly Railway Station. Janet's sobbing uncontrollably as I'm about to board the train for London on the way to Heathrow for the first leg of my journey to the British Solomon Islands Protectorate. Janet's wearing her leather coat unbelted because of a maternal bulge. Taking her in my arms, I try to console, but tears keep coming and I worry whether she's in a fit state to drive back to our home. There's another ten minutes before the train's scheduled to leave, so we board the corridor carriage together. Janet calms down a little.

'I'm not looking forward to going back to the house. There's only a camp bed there now' she blurts out between sobs.

Transition

'But you'll be going to your Mum and Dad's tomorrow. They'll look after you.' We hold hands. 'I'll write to you every week. Remember you'll be coming out at Christmas with our new baby. Try to focus on that.'

'The train on platform 3 will depart in two minutes' announces the tannoy as I help Janet out of the compartment. We have a last emotional embrace, Janet still in floods of tears. Waving through the carriage window as the train pulls out, both of us now in tears; desolate, aching eyes. My emotions are mixed. Huge sadness at leaving my loving, pregnant Wife, but also great excitement at the prospect of starting a new life in a Tropical Paradise as a Co-operatives Adviser.

* * *

Janet came out to the Solomons in January 1971 with our son Paul, only 6 weeks old; a long and arduous journey. My contract was for 2 years, but everything went so well, both job-wise and socially, that we stayed for another 4 years, returning to England in 1977. My daughter, Annette, was born in the Solomons in 1972.

I re-joined the CWS as a Distribution Centre Manager in Preston before moving to the Co-operative College near Loughborough where I joined the International Co-operative Training Centre. This enabled me to continue with overseas consultancy work including assignments in Bangladesh, Nepal, Nigeria, Thailand and Sierra Leone. The ODA also financed a study tour of Co-operatives in Kenya, Malawi, Zimbabwe, Burma and Egypt. We moved to Castle Donington, a few miles from the College, in April 1979 now with a second daughter, Sarah.

My Father died whilst I was in Bangladesh the message reaching me only after the funeral as I was in a remote village advising an Irrigation Co-operative. Mother continued to live in Colne, at 17 Temple Street, so I was now able to visit her more often.

CHAPTER 10

Reconciliation

Climbing the steep steps towards the pebble-dashed council house, I'm apprehensive. Having worked overseas for a number of years on UN assignments in Africa and Asia, I've been unable to visit Mother for some time. Dark brown paint on the wooden back door is flaking off. I try the handle, but the door's locked. At first there's no response to my loud knock, knock, knock, which echoes in the passage outside the kitchen, but after a few minutes the sound of a key being turned in the mortice lock confirms that Mother's in. It seems a struggle; the lock probably needs oiling, or maybe she's finding it more difficult to turn the large key because of arthritic hands. Slowly the door creaks open, but only as far as a security chain allows. Mother's challenging eyes peer through the dim, narrow chink.

'Who a' ye?' Mother asks, accusingly. Of course she knows who I am, but it's her way of rebuking me for not coming to see her more often. She unfastens the chain.

'You'd better come in, whoever you are', keeping up the pretence that I'm a stranger.

Mother looks small and frail. Her grey hair's frizzy; her wrinkled face has a yellowish tinge. A thin, light blue, constantly worn overall is now too big for her shrinking body. As she slowly, limpingly, leads me into the living room, I can see her left leg, bent like the frame of a cross-bow, is getting even worse. 'How long before it breaks altogether?' I ask myself. Mother damaged the leg when trying to jump on board the platform of a moving bus, the injury putting paid to her walking days with '*The Ramblers*'. Nevertheless she still refuses to use a walking stick, regarding it as 'giving in' to old age.

On the mantelpiece is a prized, framed photo of Mother with two of her Granddaughters. Beverley's wearing a bright red windcheater, Alison a blue cagoule, Mother's yellow fleece jacket's fastened up to the chin. All three have sturdy walking boots and gaily patterned

Reconciliation

woolly hats. Beverley's gloved hand rests on Grandma's shoulder, Mother smiling happily, eyes shining out of a ruddy, weather worn face. Behind are stonewalled fields with patches of snow, a bright sun unable to melt the icy ground. Beyond stands majestic Pendle Hill, dominating the landscape with its wild, brackened slopes and rocky outcrops, the winding path to the summit clearly visible. A picture of happier days out rambling in the Lancashire countryside.

A dish of potpourri on the dresser can't hide slightly pungent smells penetrating the house. Len's bought Mother a microwave oven, but she still doesn't know how to use it, resulting in a series of burnt meals lying uneaten on the kitchen table. Other food, left out of the fridge, is beginning to moulder. Mother's become incontinent; warm air absorbing the consequences of her affliction. The open hearth coal fire has long since gone, replaced by an ugly gas contraption; on at full three bars despite it being a warm day.

'Make a cup of tea, Roy' Mother demands.

I go back into the kitchen looking for teapot and mugs. They're lying on the draining board, washed but still stained from decades of use. I rewash them under the tap, drying with a damp pot towel found lying on the large stone sink.

'Have you any tea bags?' I shout from the kitchen.

'No' replies Mother in an irritated voice. 'You know I only use Co-op Indian Prince Tea. I want a proper cup. There's a new packet in the pantry.'

I follow Mother's bidding, despite knowing the tea will be far too strong, take ages to brew in the flowered, ceramic teapot, and will inevitably have tea leaves floating on the surface. The milk's gone sour, but I manage to find a tin of powdered milk. I don't put sugar in, knowing how exacting Mother is on sweetness. Sugar bowl, teapot, mugs, and milk powder are taken through into the living room on a rickety cane tray; very old, very wobbly.

Conversation's stilted as I try explaining why it's been so long since I last came to see her.

'I've been working overseas, in Nigeria and Bangladesh. For the International Labour Organisation' I tell her, thinking she might be impressed by her son helping starving people in developing countries. But it doesn't register. Her once international horizons have shrunk to Colne's borders; even the borders of 17 Temple Street.

'Sarah's doing well on the piano. She's already passed Grade 7; and she's started playing the clarinet.'

Mother's eyes light up a little at this, but soon glaze over again. I start to criticize the Tory Government, but think better of it. Mother no longer takes what is now *The Morning Star*, reading only the weekly free newspaper and *Colne Times*. She's cut herself off from politics, blocking her mind from the almost complete collapse of communism and her idealistic, utopian hopes for the working class. A copy of '*The Dalesman*' lies on the couch where I'm sitting.

'Do you have this delivered?' I ask.

'No, our Len brings it round. He comes two or three times a week and he's arranged for a cleaner to do some washing and ironing. Nobody else comes, not even Mary or Clarice.' Again I feel a pang of guilt for not visiting more often.

'Shall I put the TV on?' I ask.

'No, it's a load of rubbish, nothing but sex and violence. News is all about disasters round the world. Everybody's short of money. There's nothing but war, war, war. The capitalist system's collapsing just as Karl Marx always said it would.' Mother takes a final aim at a disintegrating World. 'The only programme I watch is '*Last of the Summer Wine*'.

I go back into the kitchen, collecting the burnt and stale food into a black plastic bag, which I find in a drawer. The outside bin's full, but I press the bag down and squeeze the lid as far as it will go. The bin mustn't have been emptied for weeks. 'I'll tell Len, he'll sort it out with the Council' I think, somewhat optimistically.

'Mum, you've hardly anything in' I shout through the living room door. 'No bread, no eggs. There's nothing at all in the fridge. We'd better go to the Co-op and stock you up.'

I'm glad of an opportunity to help. Mother puts on her long winter coat, though it's only autumn and quite warm. We go slowly down the steps, Mother reluctantly holding my arm. Helping her into my new Mini, she complains.

'Not much room in here. Why've you wasted money on a new car like this?'

The Co-op Store at the bottom of the street has long since closed, so I drive to the newish supermarket in the main road; still the Co-op, of course.

Reconciliation

'Hello, Martha, I've saved you some nice sirloin steak, and we've got lean bacon' says the meat counter supervisor.

Carlos, son of a Spanish family who came as refugees from the Spanish Civil War, was someone my Father had got a job for at the Co-op, for which he's always been grateful. Mother buys far too much. She'll never eat it, but won't be dissuaded. We walk slowly round the store buying bread, eggs, chocolate biscuits and a whole assortment of fruit and veg. The basket I'm carrying is getting quite heavy.

I stop to chat with one of the checkout girls who I recognise as daughter of an old school friend, but when I turn round, Mother's disappeared. 'I think she's gone into the toilet' explains the other checkout assistant. Paying for the groceries and packing them into two plastic bags, I wait outside the toilet door. Mother doesn't appear. Worried, I look round the store, but she's nowhere to be seen. I notice a back exit into the car park: 'Maybe she's waiting for me at the car' I reassure myself.

In the small car park there's still no sign of her, but I catch a glimpse of a long brown coat disappearing round the far corner of the store. Running across, I manage to catch her before she tries to cross the busy road.

'What's up, Mum? You can't walk all the way home from here.' She looks at me forlornly.

'I've had an accident. Can't get in your new car like this. It'll stink.'

I look at her with deep compassion, putting my arm round sagging shoulders.

'Do you really think I'd leave you stranded? What does a bit of a smell in the car matter? Let's get you home; you can have a bath.'

We walk slowly back to the car, Mother leaning on me.

* * *

I arrive at Burnley General Hospital with a heavy heart. Mother has deteriorated since my last visit and I'm apprehensive as to how she'll look and react. Visits to hospital and the family home have not always ended happily. She's been moved to another ward so I go to the Ward Matron's office to find out which. There's nobody in the office so I wait, my eyes wandering round the high ceilinged room, walls newly painted NHS cream. Several nurses are busy looking after patients in the large, regimented, ward. They wear starched white pinafore aprons over blue and white striped dresses, all perfectly tailored and neatly worn. Expertly folded cotton caps, again starched white, bob up and down as nurses lean towards patients, helping them to eat or making them comfortable. 'Nothing's too much for these hospital angels' I ponder. The ward's immaculate, with a not so subtle smell of disinfectant and carbolic; the smell of clean. A white-coated doctor comes in, surrounded by young interns. He jokes with one of the patients, who responds with a gentle laugh.

Looking over to a bed near the office, a young woman I seem to recognise waves and calls me over. Moving closer, I see she's a family friend. As newly-weds, Joy and her husband Gordon had been buddies with me and Janet. Boozy nights out at working men's clubs with 'on the edge' comedians and doubtful singers; visits to the Imperial Ballroom to see the latest Pop Groups; trips to Blackpool to see the lights and dance on the Pier; then on to the South Shore and Fun House.

'Your Mum's in ward 7', Joy says in almost a whisper. 'But she's OK.'

'What are you doing here?' I ask in a nervous voice. Joy begins to sob quietly so I pull up a chair and hold her hand gently. Recovering her composure she confides in me with her woes.

'A few weeks ago we were planning a walking holiday in France' she relates in a trembling voice. 'I'd been having pain in my hip and Gordon thought it better to have the doctor look at it before we set off on holiday.' A pause as she struggles to regain her composure. 'After examining me, the doctor sent me straight to hospital.' Joy takes a deep breath and begins to cry, tears trickling slowly down her pale cheeks. 'Roy, I have cancer.' Joy stumbles out the words. I hold her hand more tightly, but she pulls it away to wipe the tears. 'Gordon's devastated.'

I don't know what to say, but mumble hopefully.

'Perhaps it's not as bad as it seems?' But, looking into her eyes, I can see that it is. 'I'll tell Janet. I'm sure she'll want to visit.'

My mind races over the many happy times we'd shared, first as teenagers, then young newly-weds. We stay silent; silence then broken by the Ward Matron's return.

Reconciliation

'Mr Kershaw, your Mother's in ward 7. You should go up and see her. She knows you're here' the Sister instructs in a strict but compassionate tone.

The nurse in ward 7 waves as I enter. She knows our family well, being the granddaughter of my Mother's best friend.

'Over 'ere Roy' she beckons in a strong Lancashire accent. 'I'm just sittin' Martha up so ye can talk to 'er better. She's OK, but very weak.'

I grab a chair and sit next to the bed caressing Mother's hand. How painful to be holding, within an hour, the hands of two dying, much loved people.

'I'll bring ye' some tea' the nurse kindly offers. 'Is it four sugars you 'ave, Martha?'

Mother looks startled. Everyone knows she has only one and a half spoonfuls and can immediately tell the difference if there's any variation.

'Janice's only joking, Mum. She knows exactly how much sugar you have.' We all laugh and Mother's face softens.

We talk about the usual things. 'Yes, the children are doing well' I reply to Mother's first question. 'Len came to see me yesterday. Still looking for a job since Broughton's mill closed down' she tells me. 'Your cousin Barbara's passed away' she adds, sadly. 'Barbara was a wonderful girl.' We talk about other family members, of whom there are many.

Conversation drifts to a halt, but I can see Mother wants to say something. Our family seldom talk intimately, so it's a struggle to discuss deep feelings; but finally she speaks out in a quiet, yet emotional voice.

'I'm dying, Roy.' A long pause, then she continues. 'They won't let me through the Pearly Gates, though. I've never believed in God.' Mother sighs and looks down at her wrinkled, work worn hands. They're still strong hands; weaver's hands. I caress them with my soft, 'never done a day's manual work' fingers.

'I don't know whether there's a God or there isn't a God. But I do know that if Heaven exists, that's where you'll be going' I whisper. 'You've done what you think's right all your life. Unselfishly. Nobody can do more than that.' Mother doesn't respond, but she looks a little more content.

Visiting time's over. I kiss her on the cheek and return the chair to its designated place. However, instead of leaving, I go back to the end of the bed and turn to Mother, who's still awake and sitting up.

'Mum, you know me and Len love you, don't you?' The words come from I don't know where.

'Yes, I do' …. words drift from a reconciled, joyful face. Eyes sparkle; a shower of stars; a burst of sparks from a Roman Candle.

We've made our peace.

* * *

A week later the phone rings at our home in Castle Donington.

'Hello, Roy. I'm afraid your Mum's much worse. Don't think she has long to live. Please come up to the hospital as soon as you can. Sorry to have to bring you the bad news.' Nurse Janice's voice is sympathetic but professional.

'Thanks for letting me know, Janice. I'll set off straight away. Hope to be there in two hours at the most.' Janet's out, so I leave a note.

I drive north up the M1 heading towards Bradford; longer than other routes, but usually quicker. My mind swings between depression and exhilaration, making it difficult to focus on the road. Through Colne, the traffic's heavy on Burnley Road making me stressed and impatient, blasting my horn at other dawdling drivers, though it doesn't make any difference. I arrive at the hospital at four o'clock instead of the hoped for three thirty and it takes a few minutes to find a parking space. Finally I hurry into the hospital, heading for ward 7. As I enter, Janice comes rushing over.

'Dreadfully sorry, Roy, but your Mum passed away just an hour ago. She went peacefully, though. You'll find her on a hospital trolley just along the corridor. Everyone's very upset.'

I walk slowly, nervously, along the corridor. I've only once before seen a dead person, my Grandmother Ellen, and that experience had come as a shock, numbness freezing my mind and body. Aunty Annie had consoled me then, but it had still been difficult to take in. What would it now be like seeing my own Mother? However this time, looking down at her frail body, I've only warm feelings of love and gratitude. Mum's face is calmer and more serene than I've ever seen

Reconciliation

before; all anxieties have gone; all the many cares and troubles of her life have faded.

'If there is a Heaven, then that's where she is' I murmur to myself with great confidence and belief.

* * *

A few weeks later I enter the empty house on Temple Street through the back door, having taken the key from under a brick where Len's left it; not very secure but, there again, nothing much worth stealing remains. The door leads directly into the kitchen, dark and dismal despite sunlight trying to penetrate thick, dusty curtains. It's silent except for the tired buzz of a couple of flagging flies circling a bottle of sour milk on the kitchen table. There's a musty smell of a room left empty for several months.

I shuffle through the almost bare living room; piano and Welsh Dresser have gone. The clock, still standing on the mantelpiece, no longer ticks. Next to it is the Robbie Burns jug, handle broken off. A torn, discoloured sheet of music lies limp on the bare floor. Beethoven's Moonlight Sonata, Mother's favourite piece. I hadn't mastered it despite promises of financial reward: 'If you play it without those continual mistakes, I'll give you a shilling.' Never earned.

Mounting carpetless, echoing stairs I enter my parents' bedroom which, unexpectedly, has been left as it was; bed made, covered by a bright, flower-patterned flock eiderdown and clean white pillow cases. The carved, oak headboard, Mother's pride and joy, still stands guard. My mind flashes back to Sunday mornings when, as a child, I would come into Mother's bed to be told stories. Not fairy tales, but stories of fantastic journeys to exotic foreign lands. To India where sacred cows roam the streets unmolested; the Taj Mahal glitters in pale sunshine; Fakirs constantly pray to their Gods and hooded cobras dance to the snake charmer's flute. To Africa where tigers and leopards stalk unwary travellers; explorers search for King Solomon's Mines; magnificent, spear-waving natives dance to the sound of insistent drums. To New Zealand where Maoris challenge visitors with blood curdling war chants; geysers leap from the earth and there are more sheep than people. Our journeys were to be paid for by breeding angora rabbits, fur being sold at enormous prices.

On top of a tall chest of drawers, in an alcove next to the bed, still stands the large, illustrated book, *'Travellers Tales'*, from whence many of the magical stories came. Next to this lean Karl Marx's *Das Capital* and *The Communist Manifesto*. There's also a voluminous edition of *The Works of William Shakespeare* and a well-worn book of *Keats and Shelley* poems. A hard-back copy of Pearl S Buck's *The Good Earth*, from where Mother had found stories of China. Howard Fast's *Spartacus* is one source of Mother's longing for a working-class revolt and dreams of a just society where exploitation and cruelty have been eliminated. Incongruously, there's also a small Penguin paperback, *The Philanderer* by Stanley Kauffmann. 'Maybe Mum had another side to her character, not all principles and high moral standards?' I ponder.

Hanging on the wall, above the chest of drawers, is a picture of Lenin. It looks more like a photograph than a painting, being in black and white. Mother's hero strikes an intellectual rather than revolutionary pose, standing in a library, reading a book. Large, balding head, moustached with a wispy grey beard, he hardly looks the wild eyed leader of rebellious insurgents attacking the *Winter Palace* or aboard the cruiser *Aurora* inciting the crew to mutiny.

Dominating the bedroom's an impressive woven silk picture. Framed in a solid wood surround protected by a now dusty glass frontage, it hangs on the wall facing the bed. Joan of Arc is portrayed not as a meek Maid of Orleans or Martyr burning at the stake, but as a triumphant soldier dressed in shining armour, with glittering sword and grasping a triumphant banner. The image has been there for as long as I can remember; Len says I was born under its gaze. As a child I'd been fascinated by the picture, but didn't understand its significance. Looking at it now I realize the Maid of Orleans was a heroine to Mother, not because of her religious martyrdom or success in battle, but because of her indomitable spirit and courage as a poor peasant girl.

* * *

Message to Martha – sung by Adam Faith
'Spread your wings for New Orleans.

Reconciliation

> Kentucky bluebird, fly away
> And take a message to Martha, message to Martha.'

This is my Message to Martha:

Dear Mum

I'm writing this letter in the hope it will somehow reach you through the unknowable cosmos. Though our family didn't talk much, we were still deeply aware of each-others feelings, whether happy or sad. Perhaps this epistle will help put such feelings and affections into words.

The last years of your life were full of disappointment and disillusion. Idealistic visions of a Working-Class Utopia finally disintegrated with the collapse of Communism, first in Eastern Europe, then in the Soviet Union. Tearing down of the Berlin Wall; success of Solidarity in Poland; continual splits in the UK Communist Party were all symptoms of a failed ideology. Even the Co-operative Movement was on the decline, gradually losing its democratic, ethical base. Trade Union membership plummeted, their strength diminished by Government legislation, even under a Labour Government.

Perhaps this was inevitable. The British Psyche tends towards evolution, rather than revolution. Independent spirits refuse to bow to any ideology, however utopian it might seem. People want to 'go to the devil in their own way'. They want to be free to decide for themselves how to run their own lives. The fact that Communism 'just doesn't work' had been clear for many years.

But this doesn't mean your life, and Dad's, were in vain, or that you didn't both contribute greatly to making people's lives better. The lot of the Working Class improved immeasurably during your lifetime. No more starting work at twelve or thirteen. No more toiling fifty or sixty hours a week for a pittance. Conditions of employment improved immensely, with paid holidays and health and safety legislation. The Weaver's Union, and your campaigning, played a major part in this transformation - employers and capitalists wouldn't have relinquished profits and power of their own volition. It was the left that created the National Health Service which continues to benefit the working class.

Co-operatives kept the cost of living down for working people, the end of the year 'Divi' often making a big difference to family income. Your membership and steadfast loyalty helped keep the Co-op strong. You marched with the Co-operative Women's Guild, Banner on high, campaigning for women's suffrage. Remember, when you were born, women didn't have the vote. Education was an important part of Co-operative Philosophy, with Societies and the Co-operative College providing classes for adults who'd missed out on schooling. I still remember learning about Robert Owen in Colne Co-operative evening classes. It was the Left who promoted the Workers Educational Association. You played a part in all of this. Although membership always remained small, and the Communist Party had little political strength, individual Party Members such as you and dad had major impacts, punching well above your weight. In the work place, as a shop steward in the mill, you championed solidarity, speaking up for weavers' rights.

All this was done with great compassion.

At national level, communists John Cox and Gary Lefley played key roles in the Campaign for Nuclear Disarmament. You helped Manchester Party Member, Benny Rothman, lead a mass trespass on Kinder Scout to gain access to privately owned open moorland for the People.

Internationally, Communists were often involved in independence struggles against colonialist oppression with Walter Sisulu and Joe Slove prominent in the anti-apartheid movement in South Africa. Roddy Connolly, a Communist leader in the fight for Irish Independence, is another example. You always made sure I knew about these momentous events, developing in me a strong sense of social justice and compassion – and a yen to visit foreign lands.

Mum, you brought up two well adjusted, healthy (non-smoking!), and successful sons. We were encouraged to take an active part in music and sport, providing the wherewithal even when money was tight. Education was a priority, and you persevered when we were distracted by other pursuits. You never forced your political beliefs on either of us but, by example, made sure we had a social conscience. Neither Len nor I could have asked for more.

Thank You.

Your loving son, Roy

PS You stuck to your principles – always!

Made in the USA
Charleston, SC
21 November 2015